Occupational Ethics Series

Elizabeth Beardsley and John Atwell
Series Editors

7672233

BUSINESS ETHICS

Norman Bowie

Center for the Study of Values
University of Delaware

PRENTICE-HALL, INC., ENGLEWOOD CLIFFS, NEW JERSEY 07632

Library of Congress Cataloging in Publication Data

Bowie, Norman E.,
    Business ethics.

    (Occupational ethics)
    Bibliography: p.
    Includes index.
    1. Business ethics. I. Title. II. Series.
HF5387.B68   174'.4   81–12034
ISBN 0–13–095901–4   AACR2

ISBN 0-13-095901-4

©1982 by Prentice-Hall, Inc., Englewood Cliffs, N.J. 07632

Editorial/production supervision by: Marybeth Brande
Cover and interior by: Jayne Conte
Manufacturing Buyer: Harry P. Baisley

Printed in the United States of America

10 9 8 7 6 5 4 3 2 1

Prentice-Hall International, Inc., London
Prentice-Hall of Australia Pty. Limited, Sydney
Prentice-Hall of Canada, Ltd., Toronto
Prentice-Hall of India Private Limited, New Delhi
Prentice-Hall of Japan, Inc., Tokyo
Prentice-Hall of Southeast Asia Pte. Ltd., Singapore
Whitehall Books Limited, Wellington, New Zealand

to
Brian and Pete

Contents

Preface

Moral Presuppositions of Business 3   39

An Ethical Analysis of "Competition" and Consumer Sovereignty 4   66

Self-Regulation 5   89

Government Regulation 6   114

Whistle Blowing and Other Why Be Moral Questions 7   138

Prentice-Hall Series in Occupational Ethics

An increasing number of philosophers are coming to appreciate the value of making our discipline constructively available to those whose lives are chiefly focused on some form of practical activity. It is natural that philosophers specializing in ethics should be in the forefront of this movement toward "applied philosophy." In both writing and teaching, many leading ethical theorists are currently dealing with concrete issues in individual and social life.

While this change has been taking place within the philosophic community, practitioners in various fields have (for several complex reasons) turned their attention to the ethical dimensions of their own activities. Whether they work in areas traditionally called "professions" or in other occupations, they wish to consider their job-related decisions in relation to ethical principles and social goals. They rightly recognize that many, if not most, ethical problems facing all of us arise in our occupational lives: we are often expected to conduct ourselves "at work" in ways which appear to conflict with the ethical principles believed valid in other social relationships; in our occupations themselves certain normally accepted practices sometimes seem to contradict each other; in short, ethical dilemmas of enormous proportion face the morally conscientious person. Whether philosophical ethics can help resolve these acute problems is an inescapable question.

A third recent development is the growing tendency of students to think of themselves as persons who do or will have certain occupational roles. This tendency is noticeable at several stages of life—in choosing an occupation, in preparing for one already chosen, and in pursuing one that has been entered some time ago.

The convergence of these three contemporary developments has created a need for appropriate teaching materials. The *Occupational Ethics* Series is designed to meet this need. Each volume has been written by a philosopher, with the advice or collaboration of a practitioner in a particular occupation. The volumes are suitable for liberal arts courses in ethics and for programs of preprofessional study, as well as for the general reader who seeks a better understanding of a world that most human beings inhabit, the world of work.

John E. Atwell and Elizabeth L. Beardsley,
Editors

Preface

One of the most distinctive features of American society is the privately owned business enterprise. Some of these businesses are small, single proprietaries or partnerships. Most of the vast numbers of Americans who work for private companies, however, work for large corporations. This book is written for those who are employed or who are about to be employed by private companies. It is also written for the managers, executive officers, and board members of these companies. Finally, it is written for all those who are interested in business and the free enterprise system.

The book focuses on criteria for determining what constitutes ethical business practice. The public's concern with ethical practices in business is well known. Systematic treatments of business ethics are few in number, and those that do exist are not widely known. Although this is a philosophy book, I have tried to write it in such a way that its subject matter is readily available to a wide public. I presuppose no knowledge of philosophy, and I have tried to avoid philosophical jargon.

For example, in the opening chapter I take the perspective of a new employee as he or she assumes the first job. I try to show how moral obligations arise when one accepts a position with a firm, for example, an obligation to be loyal. Some of these job-related obligations help us to escape from some nasty moral dilemmas. On the other hand, some of the obligations that an employer or supervisor may try to impose on an

employee are illegitimate. I argue that some criteria are needed to sort out
the legitimate from the illegitimate ones.

One means for distinguishing legitimate from illegitimate job-related
obligations is to determine what constitutes a morally appropriate theory
of the purpose of a business firm. In Chapter 2 several models are
evaluated critically. Yet another means for distinguishing legitimate from
illegitimate job-related obligations is to see if these obligations are consistent with universal moral norms that underlie all moral institutions including business. Chapter 3 addresses this issue. Finally, an appeal to
morally acceptable standard business practice yields another criterion for
distinguishing legitimate from illegitimate job-related obligations. In
Chapter 4, two of the most common business practices—competition and
deference to consumer sovereignty—are evaluated morally. These four
chapters provide a theoretical structure for business ethics. They will not,
however, provide a handbook for settling all ethical issues that arise in
business. There is no such handbook for business or as a matter of fact for
any other area of ethics. Subscribers to any of the major ethical theories
will be disappointed. Since I do not believe that any one theory (e.g.,
utilitarianism) is adequate, this book is not written from one moral point
of view. It borrows freely from many of the great ethical traditions
whenever one tradition or another can illuminate a central issue.

Having established a theory of business ethics, I then ask how that
theory can be put into practice. Chapter 5 considers techniques of self-
regulation. Chapter 6 presents some of the pro's and con's of government
regulation. Chapter 7 addresses the question of why a business firm or
businessperson should do what is morally appropriate when they can get
away with doing what is not moral.

Readers familiar with business will recognize many of the issues
discussed within the chapters—deceptive advertising, loyalty to the firm
versus whistle blowing, stockholder interests, the profit motive, and equal
opportunity. Readers familiar with philosophy will be familiar with many
theories—Kantianism, utilitarianism, Platonism, Rawlsianism—and with
many of the issues—equal opportunity versus equal results, the problem
of why we should be moral, weakness of will, the scope of human rights,
competing theories of freedom, and the limits of law. It is my hope that
readers from both perspectives will come away from this book with a
deeper appreciation and understanding of the central issues that are referred to as business ethics.

Marxists will not be happy with this book. The book does provide
argument after argument that implies the necessity for the moral reform
of business practice. However, the book does not call for the overthrow of
the private enterprise system. No consistent Marxists will waste time
discussing possible reforms for an institution that they believe to be totally corrupt. They are entitled to their opinion. Their opinion is not mine.

I have been at work on the manuscript for three years. The manuscript benefited from much criticism—both friendly and hostile. I deeply appreciate the careful comments provided on all drafts of this book by the general editors of this series, John Atwell and Elizabeth Beardsley. One Prentice-Hall reviewer read two drafts and provided many helpful suggestions. I also appreciated the comments of Steven Cahn, Joseph Desjardins, Ronald Duska, and the anonymous Prentice-Hall reviewers. Two persons most familiar with the book are my two secretaries, Marguerite Baker and Sandy Manno. They have retyped this manuscript more times than I want to remember. The manuscript might not be finished now except for the pressure of my two boys who wanted a book dedicated to them and have wanted me to hurry up.

Norman Bowie

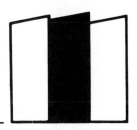

My Position
and Its Duties

The First Job

Suppose that your first job after college involves a position in the purchasing department of a medium-sized manufacturing plant. You are hired to obtain about six products, all of which are essential to the electric clocks that your firm manufactures. You report to a Mr. Norwood who has worked with this firm for ten years. Your assignment, which was detailed in the job description and in subsequent interviews, was to negotiate the best contract you could for the six products under your control. You were told specifically that it is the policy of your company *not* to give special consideration to those firms that had been awarded contracts in the past. With this information clearly in mind, you begin negotiations for a contract for the ensuing year.

One day Mr. Norwood and a sales representative from the Slow Spring Company take you to lunch. Both persons make it clear to you that Slow Spring is to get the bid. In return you will get a kickback of $10,000 and Mr. Norwood will get a kickback of $5,000. Mr. Norwood indicates that failure to cooperate will result in bad evaluations and eventual dismissal. Indeed, Mr. Norwood has a file on the person who held your job previously. It contains a set of bad evaluations and a dismissal notice. You consider informing Mr. Norwood's supervisors. Discrete inquiry, however, indicates that Mr. Norwood's supervisor is busy covering up some design flaws in the clock—a decision dictated by top management on the basis that it will be cheaper to suffer a few consumer complaints than to correct the problem—at least for this model year.

This is your first job and good first jobs are hard to get. What should you do? You face an ethical dilemma.

The Organization of This Book

This book on business ethics will not provide an answer to the dilemma just described. There are no clear-cut definitive answers to moral dilemmas. What the book will provide is a set of theoretical tools that will assist one to face intelligently and sensitively the dilemma or to prevent it if one is in a position to do so. One of the assumptions of the book is that ethical decisions in business are similar in structure to other business decisions. Of course, these ethical decisions are often very complex, open ended, and amorphous, but so are many other business decisions. In marketing or personnel management, for example, one needs to identify precisely the variables that make up the problem; one needs to decide on an acceptable solution, and then one needs to act so that the solution is achieved quickly and efficiently. Consider the decision as to whether a cereal company should introduce a new product—Crazy Stars. The company will perform a market analysis making sure that all the target populations (variables) are adequately included. On the basis of the analysis, plus considerations of start-up costs, the extent of risk, and the future economic outlook, a decision as to whether or not Crazy Stars should be marketed would be made. Once the decision is made, the various managers in the corporation will implement the decision.

The structure of a decision regarding an ethical problem—for example, should a company seek minority suppliers of a good—is similar to that of deciding whether or not to introduce a new cereal. However, when one looks to the principles for an ethical decision, one appeals to ethical theory as well as to marketing theory. The intention is to have the reader appreciate how the problems of ethics arise within business and then to understand how a rational attempt to solve these problems requires a consideration of some of the broader issues in ethical theory. Let us begin with the notion of a job description.

The Job Description

Cultural, Legal, and Moral Dimensions Within business every person has a position—assembly-line worker, sales person, accountant, public relations person, chief executive, member of the governing board. This position is defined by a set of rules or practices. In some cases there is a formal job description. In other cases the number of formal rules is minimal, but one learns one's job by observing how others do it—one learns the customs associated with the position. To begin a job is to enter a world governed by a complex set of rules, principles, and practices. A necessary condition for successful job performance is an understanding of the nature of the job itself. Any personnel manager will tell you that a common problem for employees is the unhappiness or frustration that results when a person understands the nature of what is expected but for some reason or another is dissatisfied working under that set of expectations. In sociological language, when one takes a job, one is taking on a certain role. Dorothy Emmet describes a role as follows:

> The concept of a role is . . . one which enters into the sociologists' account of a social interaction. It is needed in describing the repeatable patterns of social relations which are not mere physical facts and which are structured partly by the rules of acceptable behavior in the society in question.[1]

The philosopher R. S. Downie puts it this way: "A role in the relevant sense . . . is a cluster of rights and duties with some sort of social function."[2] A role is more or less determinate, depending upon the kind of rules that govern the behavior. Sometimes roles are governed simply by implicit understandings, maxims, or rules of thumb, referred to in this book as the customary elements of a role. At other times there are more formal and explicit rules governing a role, referred to in this book as the legal elements of a role. Finally, certain rules governing a role may have moral force attached to them, referred to as the moral elements of a role. Because most roles are governed by a number of rules, it is not uncommon to find a role that has customary, legal, and moral elements.

Our vocational roles contain customary, legal, and moral elements. The legal elements are explicit formal rules and regulations that serve as the job description or the job responsibilities that one must follow if one is to keep the job. To put it another way, failure to live up to the legal rules is legitimate grounds for dismissal. Usually legal elements surrounding a job include the number of hours one is to work, the starting and ending times, and most important the goal or goals that one is to accomplish. Within unionized industries, these legal elements are spelled out in the collective bargaining agreement. In an automobile assembly plant, a worker will be paid X dollars per hour for forty hours per week to attach doors to auto bodies where the assembly line is to operate at twenty finished automobiles per hour.

The job description is clearly not exhausted by its legal elements, however. A new person on the assembly line quickly learns that there are customs governing both how one does the job and how one interacts with

---

[1] Dorothy Emmet, *Rules, Roles, and Relations* (Boston: Beacon Press, 1966), p. 15.

[2] R. S. Downie, *Roles and Values. An Introduction to Social Ethics* (London: Methuen & Co. Ltd., 1971), p. 128.

colleagues. The new employee learns the "etiquette" surrounding a job. Failure to follow job etiquette does not provide legitimate grounds for dismissal, but it does make one's relations with one's colleagues unpleasant. If the violations of job etiquette are serious enough, one's colleagues will find ways to drive the new employee out or get him or her fired. A person entering the job market should not underestimate the constraints that job etiquette puts on individual behavior. Sometimes the customary elements surrounding a job provide more constraints than do the legal elements.

It is obvious from the foregoing remarks that following the legal rules and conforming to the job etiquette is in one's self-interest. Such behavior is prudent behavior, and for many persons self-interest is motivation enough. One will note, however, that the language of most job descriptions includes moral injunctions. One ought to do one's job well. One ought to be loyal to the company. One ought to respect one's colleagues. Such injunctions do not appeal to self-interest but rather to the moral notion of duty. *Suppose that one could get away with not doing one's job very well or with not being respectful to one's colleagues. Moreover, suppose that it is in one's self-interest to avoid such responsibilities when one could get away with it.* Morality requires that you have a duty to do your job well and to respect your colleagues even when you could get away with it.

The moral elements of one's job are not purely descriptive. Being a good bricklayer and being six feet tall are not the same kind of statement. Being six feet tall is a simple fact about a person. If someone doubts whether Jones is six feet tall, an appropriate measuring should settle the dispute. Being a good bricklayer involves normative components as well. Just because Jones is a member of the bricklayer's union, there is nothing inconsistent in a disgruntled homeowner's saying, "I don't care if Jones does have his union card, he's no bricklayer." After a moment's reflection this distinction will not provide any mystery to students. All students know professors certified by their college or university as teachers but who, in the opinion of the students, aren't teachers at all.

Hence, to begin a job is to enter into a social institution and thereby to be under a series of norms for adequate performance. Perhaps an analogy with parenthood would make this point clearer. One is designated "a parent" either by being the mother or father of a child or by legally adopting a child. But surely the biological or legal facts do not exhaust the matter. Being a parent brings with it obligations and responsibilities. One's stewardship as a parent can be judged against one's performance in carrying out one's obligations and responsibilities. Some parents are better than others. The extensive and willful neglect of one's parental responsibilities is universally branded as immoral. Being a parent involves having a certain station in life, and with that station certain duties are associated. As it is with parenthood so also is it with one's job. "Once one has assumed the role, it binds with obligations of right and wrong."[3] In other words, people have obligations as a part of their job and what people ought to do depends in part on the jobs they have.

The popular view that having a job brings with it certain moral duties has deep roots in ethical theory. Greek philosophy of the Platonic and Aristotelian schools did not emphasize the concept of duty, but it did interpret the notion of good in a way that enables us to argue that the Greeks are legitimate forebearers of the "my station and its duties" philosophy. For Aristotle and Plato a good X is an X that adequately performs its function. A good racehorse has the characteristics that enable it to win races. A good knife is one that is sharp enough to cut effectively. To know if some object is good, it is necessary to know the function of objects of that type.

Part of what it means to be a good person is to be a person who performs the obligations associated with his or her job (function). But our roles are not limited to jobs. If one is a parent, one ought to fulfill the duties of parenthood, and in fulfilling those duties one is a good parent. If one is a bricklayer, one ought to fulfill those duties associated with the trade of bricklaying, and by fulfilling those duties one is a good bricklayer. Part of being a good person is carrying out the obligations and responsibilities of his or her various roles. Although exaggerating, the philosopher F. H. Bradley put it this way: "There is nothing better than my station and its duties, nor anything higher or more truly beautiful."[4]

Implications It may not seem that this discussion of my station and its duties has much practical import for persons on the job, but this is not so. The recognition that in taking a job one is taking on moral responsibilities is important in counteracting the view that one's job is simply an economic relation defined as an equilibrium of competing self-interests between the employer and the employee.

Consider an assembly worker who is receiving a weekly wage of $350 for forty hours of piece work. If the relation of the assembly-line worker to his or her employer is simply economic, what incentive does the worker have for quality control? The worker would like high compensation for relatively few hours of work; the employer would prefer low compensation. Each is well aware of the attitude of the other. In such a situation, the worker would consider the job as simply a job. The worker

---

[3] Charles Fried, *Right and Wrong* (Cambridge, Mass.: Harvard University Press, 1978), p. 168.

[4] F. H. Bradley, *Ethical Studies* (Indianapolis, Ind.: The Bobbs-Merrill Co., Inc., 1951), p. 136.

would view it with indifference or even hostility; the temptation would be to do as little as possible. Inevitably this attitude would have bad effects either on the products produced or on interpersonal relationships where the person holding the job interacts with a public.

These theoretical considerations seem to have some basis in fact. It is not uncommon for ordinary conversation to focus on the shoddiness of products or on the rudeness of employees dealing with the public. This point is made by the popular complaint that people no longer take pride in their work.

If one recognizes, however, that any job brings with it a set of responsibilities and duties, and if one adopts the moral point of view, then a job can never be viewed simply as a job. Economic bargaining certainly remains important, but the employee also has a duty to do the job well and the employer has a duty to provide a good salary and safe pleasant working conditions.

This concern with service and quality is most explicit in those jobs we call professions. Emmet describes a profession as follows:

> A profession . . . carries with it the notion of a standard of performance, it is not only a way of making a living, but one in which the practitioners have a fiduciary trust to maintain certain standards. These are partly standards of competence, or technical ability in carrying out functions valued in the society. But not only so: professional competence has to be joined with professional integrity. . . . A professional man carries out his functions in relation to people who also stand in a particular role relation to him. The relationship carries specific obligations, to be distinguished from those of purely personal morality, or from general obligations to human beings as such.[5]

The more professional a job, the greater the responsibilities that go with it. The Harvard Business School has its motto—To Make Business a Profession. In committing itself to that motto, the Harvard Business School commits itself to educating persons entering business in the obligations and responsibilities of a profession.

But why do greater obligations fall on professionals? The practitioner of a profession exercises a special technical skill on behalf of a client—a skill that the client needs but does not possess. Traditionally, the professional skill is a service skill, specifically a skill that benefits humankind. Doctors, lawyers, teachers, and the clergy exercise a special skill for the benefit of human beings. To exercise a skill for the benefit of humankind places the professional in a special moral relation with his or her clients. After all, if it is morally praiseworthy to serve others and one's job

---

[5] Emmet, *Rules, Roles, and Relations*, p. 159.

is to serve others, then failure to perform one's professional role diminishes one's claim to the respect and praise that attends the practice of the profession.

Although many jobs do not have as part of their job description service on behalf of others, nearly all jobs have an impact on other people. The auto assembly person who places the door on its hinges is in a moral relationship with those who purchase his or her company's line of cars. The person who purchases the car assumes that the doors were attached with care. A carelessly hung door that detaches itself from the auto body and results in injury to the occupant is an event capable of being evaluated morally. The careless person has committed a morally blameworthy act. Whenever shoddy work can injure the unwary purchaser of a product, there is an obvious moral responsibility to avoid shoddy work.

But what about garbage collectors and bus boys? Careless performance on their part is usually not dangerous, although careless performance may be messy. Even here it can be argued that there are moral obligations associated with the jobs—albeit of a much more minor nature. To needlessly cause annoyance and inconvenience is morally blameworthy as well.

Nearly every job places you in morally relevant relations with other people. The extent and stringency of the moral responsibilities associated with your job depends on the type of job that you have—very stringent for professionals, much less stringent for garbage collectors and bus boys.

A second implication that results from taking the ethics of "my station and its duties" as the starting point of business ethics is the importance of each employee's having an accurate and complete job description. Without an accurate and complete job description, an employee cannot be certain what his or her duties are. Far too often, disputes about job performance arise as a result of misunderstandings and misinformation about job expectations and methods of evaluation. Often, young women were placed in "management training positions" where the first assigned tasks were clerical and secretarial. That's where their management training ended. The job was really not a management training position at all. Precise job descriptions that are accessible publicly might help prospective employees to make vocational choices more accurately. On a less serious note, some secretaries have justified not making coffee on the basis that such chores do not fall within a secretary's job description. In any case, a necessary condition for developing the ethics of "my station and its duties" is as clear a definition of the job one holds as is possible. Only in this way can ambiguity about one's responsibilities be reduced.

A third implication of adopting the ethics of "my station and its duties" is that certain problems within business ethics have a better framework for resolution. Consider the following two cases:

_____ **The Engineering Consultant**[6] _____

As an engineering consultant to mining firms, Surestrike Mining hires you to evaluate one of its producing mines. You do so and discover that the mine has moved under adjacent property owned by West Virginia Mining Co. Hence, Surestrike does not have mineral rights to the coal being mined.

You report to Surestrike that it is infringing on the mineral rights of West Virginia Mining. Management thanks you and pays you. Six months later you discover that Surestrike is still mining under that property and that it has not notified West Virginia Mining of your findings. Your contract with Surestrike provided that you would not disclose any findings to a third party. What should you do?

_____ **Whistle Blowing—Alpha Corporation** _____

You are purchasing manager for Alpha Corporation. You are responsible for buying two $1 million generators. Your company has a written policy prohibiting any company buyer from receiving a gratuity in excess of $50 and requiring that all gratuities be reported. The company has no company policy regarding *whistleblowing*. A salesperson for a generator manufacturer offers to arrange it so that you can buy a $12,000 car for $4,000. The car would be bought from a third party. You decline the offer.

Do you now report it to your superior? To the salesperson's superior?

The ethical problems presented in cases like these would be very difficult to resolve on the basis of the traditional general theories of normative ethics alone—a contention that cannot be proved until we discuss specific normative ethical theories later in the book. However, by taking the perspective of role morality, the issues at hand are much more manageable. The question we should ask is, "What are the moral duties that go with the job of auditor, consultant, and purchasing manager?" Once that question is settled, then a defensible, albeit still debatable, answer to the question of what one ought to do is in hand.

Let us consider the case of Alpha Corporation. If the purchasing manager had accepted the gratuity, the action would have violated both company policy and common morality, and hence it would have been wrong. In addition, if Alpha Corporation had had a policy requiring whistle blowing, the manager would have acted wrongly to have violated company policy by remaining silent. But there is no such explicit policy. One may then ask whether there is an unofficial policy (the cultural element of

---

[6] These two cases are taken from material developed by the Committee for Education in Business Ethics under a grant from the National Endowment for the Humanities.

8

a job role) that requires whistle blowing. Many of my associates in business who have considered this case have indicated that such an unofficial policy does indeed exist in their companies. To the extent that such an unofficial policy does exist, then there is some moral obligation not to remain silent. Should there be neither an official nor an unofficial policy in favor of whistle blowing, then the moral obligation to whistle blow must be an obligation that is outside one's role as purchasing manager. But as shall be argued, there is no general nonrole-related obligation to blow the whistle on attempted wrongdoing.

Similar considerations arise in the case of the engineering consultant. His job was to evaluate the mine, which he did. His report included the disclosure of Surestrike's infringement on the property of West Virginia Mining. Is it part of the job of a consultant to get his or her employers to act morally? Where could we find an answer to that question? An obvious place to start is with the code of ethics of the society that represents professional engineers. If such a rule appeared in the code, then the engineer has a significant reason for believing that he has an obligation to blow the whistle on Surestrike. If the rule does not appear, the issue is more cloudy.

This discussion is not merely academic. After the Equity Funding scandal, among others, the accounting profession was under severe criticism for not exposing fraudulent client practices. Public pressure has been extensive in trying to influence both an amendment to the code of ethics of accountants and in developing an unofficial expectation that accountants would make public fraudulent activities of the firms that they audit. In this case public expectations of the moral elements of the accountant's role are becoming more stringent. In Chapter 5 much more will be said about what a code of ethics should contain and what function codes of ethics have in securing morally appropriate business practice.

However, once we move beyond the obligations associated with the role of an engineer, the appeal must be made to general moral expectations. There may be an expectation that people will report felonies, and Surestrike's infringement might be a felony. However, there is no universal obligation to influence others to behave morally. Arguments from political philosophy—the classic one being found in Locke—support the view that the enforcement of morality based on law rests primarily with the state rather than with each individual member of the state. Even the most extreme libertarians, for example, Robert Nozick, accept the view that the enforcement of legal morality is the function of the state. Property rights and contract rights are intimately bound up with laws. Moral requirements not enforced through legal sanctions may be the responsibility of the church or the family or of one's supervisor if they are of a role variety, but there seems to be no general obligation upon each person to influence everyone else to behave morally. Hence, often, but not always, role obligations are the appropriate obligations to appeal to when one is deciding what one ought to do. In the cases presented, the right thing to do is a function of the responsibilities associated with the role.

Justification of the Role Morality Approach

It has been argued that in taking a job one assumes duties, responsibilities, and obligations that are attached to the vocational role that one assumes. In considering questions of justification, it is important that a number of issues be kept distinct. Consider the following:

1. How can the view that there are duties attached to roles—especially duties attached to one's occupational role—be justified?
2. How can one justify the specific duties that are attached to specific roles?
3. What ought one to do when the duties of various roles come into conflict?
4. Is there a higher morality that supersedes role morality?

The first question asks whether or not legitimate obligations can be attached to roles. In answering this question we will call upon both of the great traditions in ethical theory—the deontological and the utilitarian. We will also discuss some of the more fundamental abstract issues that arise when one asks for justification in ethics.

Deontological Ethics One of the great traditions in ethical theory has the awkward name "deontological." This word is derived from the Greek term meaning duty. The central thesis of deontological ethics is that, in considering what one ought or ought not to do, the issue is not decided by simply determining which action has the most desirable consequences. Among the appropriate considerations are such things as the promises, the contracts, and the agreements that one makes and the relations one has to those affected by one's actions. Suppose that the chief executive of a corporation is asked to make a sizable donation on the company's behalf to a university. What should he or she do? A deontologist would argue that among other things the chief executive must also consider both past agreements (has the company promised to support this institution) and the relation this company has to the university (are many of its employees graduates? does the company use the resources of the university?). Only when all these considerations are weighed can one begin to answer the questions of what one ought to do.

Hence, according to deontological ethical theory, the relationship that one has to those affected by one's actions is a relevant consideration in determining what one ought to do. In assuming a job (a role), one assumes special relations with one's employer and colleagues and as a result assumes obligations to his or her employer or colleagues that one does not have to all workers or to all employees. In other words, a deontologist would insist that one's role is a relevant factor in considering what one ought or ought not to do. But, a critic might persist, what justifies the deontologist in selecting roles as one of the items to be considered in determining one's obligations? To this question there are a number of possible answers.

Many would argue that the starting point for justification in ethics is with what might be called moral phenomena—with the moral language that people use and the moral practices that people adopt. Ethical theories should explain the phenomena. Now both our moral language and our moral practices support the contention that at least some moral obligations arise as a result of the roles or positions one has. Being a parent does impose obligations on the parent. Deontological ethical theory incorporates society's view of the importance of role or station as an element in deciding the actual obligations one has.

Utilitarian Ethics Another justification for role morality is provided by the other great tradition in ethical theory—the utilitarian tradition. For a utilitarian, what one ought to do is determined solely by the consequences that result. One ought to act so as to bring about the best consequences one can. A utilitarian would argue that the assumption of role obligations by individuals holding the roles leads to good consequences. Again consider parenthood. It is a practical impossibility to be equally concerned with all the world's children. Children as a whole would be better off if parents were given primary responsibilities for the care of the children they had. Hence, the view that the parent role places special obligations to one's own children is justified on utilitarian grounds. So it is with other positions. Role morality is justified because that approach to morality leads to good consequences.

By justifying the position that there are moral duties attached to some roles, we have not proved that there are moral duties attached to all roles, particularly to our roles as jobholders. However, such a justification is not especially difficult given the theoretical issues discussed. A justification for job-related role morality would proceed in the same way. Utilitarians would argue on behalf of the good consequences that result; indeed, some of these alleged good consequences have already been mentioned in this chapter, for example, as an aid in resolving problems in business ethics. Nonutilitarians would appeal to the data of the moral life, specifically to moral language and moral practice to make their case. Both support the view that there is a morality associated with the jobs one holds. At this point the ball is on the critic's side of the court. The critic must show that there is something special about one's vocational role that would exempt it from having moral obligations attached while all other roles do have moral obligations attached. Until this has been done, we are justified in arguing that business ethics at least begins with one's position and its accompanying duties. At least part of what it means to be a good businessperson is to fulfill the responsibilities of one's job.

However, in justifying the relevance of "my station and its duties" to business ethics, we have not discussed the specific duties attached to roles in business and how can the specific duties be justified? Obviously, in this short book it is not possible to discuss individual vocations. The individual moral responsibilities of the butcher, the baker, and the candlestick maker cannot be spelled out in detail. Happily such a detailed discussion is not necessary. Theoretical considerations concerning the nature and function of the business enterprise itself can provide a good, but not conclusive, test for the legitimacy of any specific job-related duty. The test would go something like this: Any specific job-related duty is a legitimate duty only if that duty is consistent with the nature and function of the business enterprise itself and with universal moral norms. Thus, if the function of business is to make a profit, it cannot be a role-related moral duty of a chief executive to donate all a company's profits to charity. Chapter 2 will provide a lengthy discussion of the theories concerning the nature and function of business. The remainder of this chapter and most of Chapter 3 will provide the argument that role obligations must be consistent with universal moral norms.

Limitations of Role Morality in Business Ethics

The remaining two questions concerning the justification of role morality cannot be answered within the framework of role morality. This failure will point out some of the limitations of role morality in business ethics.

One of our remaining questions asks, "What ought one to do when the duties of various roles come into conflict?" One who asks this question realizes that a central problem of role morality is that one's role-related obligations come into conflict. The possibilities for conflict are myriad. Some conflicts arise internally within the job description itself. At the beginning of this chapter, a distinction was made among the cultural, legal, and moral components of any job. In addition to the official "employer-stated" expectations concerning job performance, there are also the unofficial "culturally based" expectations of one's colleagues or co-workers. Frequently, the official "employer" expectations come into conflict with the unofficial "co-worker" expectations. Management encourages maximum productivity. From that perspective, the best employee is the most productive employee. Co-workers hardly ever have much praise for the extraordinarily productive worker. A person who far exceeds the average is a serious threat. Management will soon wonder why others cannot produce as much. The pressure of less productive co-workers on extremely productive ones is enormous. Most highly productive workers succumb and their productivity falls. How should such conflicts be resolved?

Other conflicts occur between one's responsibilities to one's job and one's other role-related responsibilities, for example, to one's family, church, and state. These conflicts are particularly acute for young executives and persons whose job responsibilities are open ended such as doctors, lawyers, real estate agents, and university professors. A university professor could literally spend all his or her waking hours working—research is an open-ended task. Like housework, it is never done. Many jobs are like that. The more time one spends on the job, the less time one has available for other pursuits—many of which can also make moral demands on one's time.

The discussion of these conflicts is not the idle fantasizing of a philosopher—the discussion mirrors historical circumstances. Until recently, many corporations moved young executives from one part of the country to the other with great frequency, often at great emotional cost to spouses and children. Some cabinet officials in both Democratic and Republican administrations pride themselves on their sixteen-hour-a-day, seven-day-a-week work-loads and expect immediate subordinates to follow a similar routine. Some corporations have placed restraints on the kinds of activities employees may pursue in off hours. These restraints apply both to political and to social activities. Certain residential areas are preferred to others. Expectations exist concerning the amount and style of entertaining. Of course, some persons give too little to their jobs and hence fail to fulfill reasonable responsibilities, but other persons give far too much to their jobs and hence fail to meet other obligations. How are the conflicting obligations to be balanced?

Yet a final question remains concerning the justification of role morality. Is there a higher morality that supersedes role morality in any of its forms? Such a question is extremely important in any contemporary discussion of business ethics. One of the chief duties of an employee is loyalty to the employer. Many businesspersons consider loyalty the chief duty of any employee.

Although the virtue of loyalty does not receive much discussion in university circles, business people continually stress its importance. A few philosophers have taken it seriously. One of the most extensive analyses of loyalty was provided by the idealist philosopher Josiah Royce. In Royce's view, loyalty is one of those virtues that enables us to realize more fully the human potential within us. An isolated individual can never fully develop as a person. The healthy personality only develops in interaction with other personalities. A fully developed *individual* matures within society and social relations.

One way in which the interaction of a developing person and the social relations that sustain him or her can blossom is through the virtue of loyalty. As Royce put it,

> Loyalty, then, fixes our attention upon some one cause, bids us look without ourselves to see what this unified cause is, shows us thus some one plan of action, and then says to us, "In this cause is your life, your will, your opportunity, your fulfillment." . . . Loyalty has its domestic, its religious, its commercial, its professional forms, and many other forms as well. The essence of it, whatever forms it may take, is, as I conceive the matter, this: Since no man can find a plan of life by merely looking within his own chaotic nature, he has to look without, to the world of social conventions, deeds, and causes. Now, a loyal man is one who has found, and who sees, neither mere individual fellowmen to be loved or hated, nor mere conventions, nor customs, nor laws to be obeyed, but some social cause, or some system of causes, so rich, so well knit, and, to him, so fascinating, and withal so kindly in its appeal to his natural self-will, that he says to his cause: "Thy will is mine and mine is thine."[7]

With some proper changes in wording, Royce's characterization of virtue could serve as the basis for a corporate executive's speech on the importance of employee loyalty to the company where he or she works. One's work does take on meaning when one has great loyalty to the company.

Nonetheless, loyalty is loyalty to something. Suppose that one is loyal to an immoral cause or end. There is even loyalty among thieves. One should be loyal; but the object of one's loyalty should be morally appropriate. The virtue of loyalty does not require that one accept blindly the person or cause to which one is loyal. To be loyal to an employer does not require that the employee should do what the employer says come what may. Regrettably, however, it is just this kind of blind loyalty that some employers demand. Examples come immediately to mind of executives being asked to lie about product quality, delivery dates, or estimated costs of future prices. Employees sometimes are asked to carry out negative racist, sexist, ageist, or ecological policies or processes when they have value commitments that contradict such policies or processes. In portions of the business system, an institutionalized program of rebates, "kickbacks," and "considerations" remains that many employees find morally repugnant, yet they are asked to carry out the *sub rosa* policies. Engineers sometimes comment about the professional and personal anger and anxiety they feel at being asked to design products that they know to be deficient in a number of ways.[8]

---

[7] Josiah Royce, *The Philosophy of Loyalty* (New York: Macmillan Publishing Co., Inc., 1908), pp. 42–48.

[8] James A. Wilson, "Morality and the Contemporary Business System," *Journal of Contemporary Business*, Vol. 4 (Summer 1975), 48.

Even more regrettable is the fact that much of this distorted view of loyalty is written into the law itself.

> *Broadly speaking the common law says that an employee is an agent who is bound to be obedient and loyal to his or her principal, that is to the employer or boss who, acting within the authorities given him by the employer, directs the employee at work. Sections 383 and 385 of the Restatement of Agency (as revised in 1958), which is the most authoritative summary of the law in this field, state that an agent has a duty to obey all "reasonable" directions of the principal. . . . To leave absolutely no doubt that employers and union managers can demand complete loyalty from subordinates and get it, the common law says the employer may discharge his employee at any time for any reason, so long as there is no statute or agreement limiting such right of discharge. A fortiori, the employer can transfer, promote, demote, or otherwise change an employee's status at any time. It does not matter if the boss is arbitrary or even wrong in taking such action. He doesn't have to give a good reason or any reason.*[9]

But what if an employer makes unethical or illegal requests? Consider the example at the beginning of this chapter. Is Jones entitled to loyalty? In general, should an employee be loyal and carry out the requests? Not if there are universal moral norms that supersede the duties associated with one's role.

Regrettably, however, some empirical research shows that some cases of business immorality are the result of businesspersons' following role-dictated moral principles when in fact they should be following these universal norms. In a perceptive paper, J. Scott Armstrong contends that many managers in American business operate from the stockholder role. The stockholder role can be characterized as follows:

> *The stockholder role advocates that the manager distributes rewards to maximize the returns to the stockholder. Since the market is generally imperfect, decisions to maximize the benefits to the stockholder can often be accomplished at the expense of other interest groups. . . . The stockholder role encourages the manager to create situations where one party gains at the expense of another.*[10]

Armstrong then argues on the basis of psychological experiments, attitude surveys, and documented case histories that persons in the stockholder role frequently could be expected to harm third parties to maximize stockholder returns. For example, Armstrong reports on a study by Kirshnan who asked subjects what they would do in a case where an

---

[9] David W. Ewing, *Freedom Inside the Organization: Bringing Civil Liberties to the Workplace* (New York: E. P. Dutton & Co., Inc., 1977), p. 30.

[10] J. Scott Armstrong, "Social Irresponsibility in Management," *Journal of Business Research*, Vol. 5 (September 1977), 187–188.

engineer was fired for refusing to "edit" the results of a product liability survey to enable a company to receive an order. The engineer had also informed the customer on the actual results that resulted in the loss of the order. Almost two thirds of the respondents said that the company should not reinstate the engineer.[11]

Armstrong's solution is to change the nature of the management's role. Rather than subscribe to a "stockholder" role, management should subscribe to a "stakeholder" role. In Armstrong's view, management under the stakeholder role views itself as responsible to all those, but only those, groups that are affected by the firm's actions. Under the stakeholder role, management has responsibilities to many constituencies.

Before taking that step, however, we should examine the whole notion of role morality. Perhaps the difficulties run deeper than substituting one role for another. Perhaps this entire discussion can be summarized in the following sentence: Business ethics begins with the duties associated with one's role in business, but business ethics certainly does not end there. A full theory of business ethics must determine which specific duties associated with one's role are legitimate, when the duties associated with one's business role ought to be superseded by duties associated with other roles one might hold, and finally when the demands of morality not associated in any way with roles supersede the morality of roles. In the next chapter the first of these important issues will be addressed.

---

[11] Ibid., p. 191. The Kirshnan study may be found in *Academy of Management Journal*, Vol. 16 (1973), 658–669.

The Purpose
of a Corporation

At the conclusion of Chapter 1, we saw that the moral requirements placed on us in our capacity of holding a specific job could come into conflict. Our colleagues might require behavior at variance with the legal requirements of the job. A supervisor might require, in the name of obedience or loyalty, the performance of an immoral act (e.g., doctoring test results). In other words, the morality of my station and its duties is not sufficient for developing a complete theory of business ethics. In this chapter we take the first step in devising a broader theory of business ethics.

In ordinary conversation, we often make reference to a good knife, a good racehorse, or a good investment. In going to the grocery store, we want to pick out a good head of lettuce and get a good buy at the meat counter. Suppose that we were asked to explain our use of "good" in each of these contexts. We would answer the question by appealing to the functions or purpose of the thing or activity in question. For example, a good knife is sharp so that it can fulfill its function of cutting well. A good head of lettuce has those qualities that make it good to eat. There seems to be a connection between being a good X and X's fulfilling its function.

As we saw in Chapter 1, early Greek philosophy built an entire ethical theory on this insight. Both Plato and Aristotle agreed that a good X is an X that fulfills its function or purpose. Just as knives, racehorses, and investments had purposes, so did human beings, institutions, and even states. The purpose of human beings was to develop and to integrate all human capacities. In Plato and Aristotle's view, a person's rational capacities held the most important place in the process of integration and development.

Suppose that we were to apply this way of thinking to corporations. We would first ask what the function or purpose of a corporation is. Upon answering that question we would have one means for resolving internal conflicts that appear when we try to apply the morality of "my station and its duties" to business obligations. Morality would require that we perform those acts most in conformity with the purpose of a business enterprise. In other words, a statement on the purpose of a corporation would provide one, but only one, theoretical test for determining which aspects of a job description are morally adequate and which ones are not.

The Classical Theory of the Function of the Corporation

Perhaps the best known view on the function of the corporation is the one that asserts that the function of the corporation is to maximize profits for the shareholders. The economists Milton Friedman and Theodore Levitt are articulate advocates for that point of view. In the classical view, the behavior of a corporation is right when its activities seek to maximize profits and wrong when they do not.

What reasons can be given for classical definition of a corporation's function? First, that definition had been established as a precedent in law. At first the courts interpreted "maximize profits" in a very narrow sense. In the famous case of *Dodge v. Ford Motor Co.* (1919), the court required Henry Ford to increase the dividends he paid to his stockholders. The court overturned management decisions made by Ford on the grounds that stockholder rights had been violated.

> *The record, and especially the testimony of Mr. Ford, convinces that he has to some extent the attitude towards shareholders of one who has disposed and distributed to them large gains and that they should be content to take what he chooses to give. His testimony creates the impression, also, that he thinks the Ford Motor Company has made too much money, has had too large profits, and that although large profits might still be earned, a sharing of them with the public by reducing the price of the output of the company, ought to be undertaken. . . . There should be no confusion (of which there is evidence) of the duties which Mr. Ford conceives that he and the stockholders owe to the general public and the duties which in law he and his co-directors owe to protesting, minority stockholders. A business corporation is organized and carried on primarily for the profit of the stockholders. The powers of the directors are to be employed for that end. The discretion of directors is to be exercised in the choice of means to attain that end and does not extend to a change in the end itself, to the reduction of*

profits or to the nondistribution of profits among stockholders in order to devote them to other purposes.[1]

Later the courts seemed to overrule the precedent of *Dodge v. Ford Motor Co.* In the classic case *A. P. Smith Manufacturing Co. v. Barlow* (1953), the court permitted charitable donations to Princeton University. Although *A. P. Smith* is widely regarded as revolutionizing the flexibility of corporate managers and boards to seek ends beyond profits, a careful reading of the judge's opinion suggests an evolution rather than a revolution. The presiding judge still accepted the view that the function of a corporation was to maximize profits, but it was long-run profits rather than immediate profits that should count. Judge Stein's opinion is worth quoting at length.

> *I cannot conceive of any greater benefit to corporations in this country than to build, and continue to build, respect for and adherence to a system of free enterprise and democratic government, the serious impairment of either of which may well spell the destruction of all corporate enterprise. Nothing that aids or promotes the growth and service of the American university or college in respect of the matter here discussed can possibly be anything short of direct benefit to every corporation in the land. The college-trained men and women are a ready reservoir from which industry may draw to satisfy its need for scientific or executive talent. It is no answer to say that a company is not as benefited unless such need is immediate. A long-range view must be taken of the matter. A small company today might be under no imperative requirement to engage the services of a research chemist or other scientist, but its growth in a few years may be such that it must have available an ample pool from which it may obtain the needed service.*[2]

Since this decision, corporations have moved with increasing boldness into activities that clearly reduce profits in the short run. However, the law requires that corporations be prepared to show that any activity enhances long-term profits.

The Utilitarian Defense

Another defense of the classical view of the purpose of the corporation rests on the ethical theory known as utilitarianism. As you will recall, utilitarianism asserts that all ethical decisions are ultimately to be decided on the basis of consequences. Of any set of possible actions, that ac-

---

[1] *Dodge v. Ford Motor Company* (S. Ct. Mich. 1919) 204 Mich. 459.

[2] *A. P. Smith Manufacturing Company v. Barlow* Atlantic Reporter 97 A2d 186. Professor Herbert Nelson of Canisius College has reminded me that Judge Stein's decision in *A. P. Smith v. Barlow* was appealed. In upholding the appeal, Judge Jacobs seems to go further than Judge Stein in moving toward a broader view of corporate responsibility.

tion should be chosen that in all likelihood will maximize good consequences. Since corporations are not live organisms but rather are creations of the state, the state decided what the purpose of the corporation should be. Using the utilitarian framework and some empirical hypotheses about human nature, both law and government held the view that good consequences would most likely be maximized if the purpose of a corporation was to maximize profits.

These empirical hypotheses concerning human nature that contributed to the contention that corporations struggling to maximize profits will achieve the public good deserve special comment. One of the assumptions is that men and women are motivated primarily, if not solely, by self-interest. People's main concern is looking out for number one—or number one plus immediate relatives. The theory of motivation described here is given the name *psychological egoism*. In discussing psychological egoism, it should be emphasized that psychological egoism is not to be identified either with the view that humans are motivated to seek instant gratification or with the view that all humans are motivated by selfish impulses. Enlightened egoists know that tonight's drinking party is followed by tomorrow's headache and that selfish behavior is usually self-defeating and hence imprudent. In other words, enlightened egoists are often socially responsible, well-behaved people.

Another empirical hypothesis associated with the utilitarian defense is exhibited in Adam Smith's doctrine of the invisible hand. The classical economist Adam Smith (1723–1790) recognized that not all interests of all individuals could be achieved. People cannot have everything they want. Inevitably there is competition among people as they try to achieve their interests. So long as there is a government to enforce the rules of the competitive game, the competitive process is orderly and efficient. Since people look after their own interest more effectively than they look after the interests of others, the rule-governed competitive struggle will lead to the greatest good for the greatest number. In this way one can say that enlightened self-interest (egoism) constrained by limited government leads to utilitarian results.

By making these two empirical assumptions explicit, one can now see why competition has been valued positively in business culture. Business recognizes that the material goods and services that people desire neither exist ready made in nature nor are they available in great abundance. Material goods must be produced from scarce commodities. Since the means for satisfying our desires are scarce, efficiency in production is highly valued. A competitive situation in which individuals struggle against one another to satisfy their interests will be most efficient. In a competitive system where goods and services are not provided but rather are earned, people will have an incentive not only to work but to work hard. Competition molds character and contributes to utilitarian results.

Welfare, on the other hand, promotes sloth, which is dangerous to the public good.

In summarizing this point, the classical view that a corporation's purpose is to maximize profits rests on a utilitarian ethical base. Utilitarian moral philosophers argue that institutions should be designed to maximize good consequences. If it is true that human motivation has the character of enlightened self-interest and if the invisible hand operating through a rule-governed competitive process really works, then as corporations seek to maximize profits, the greatest public good will result.

The Argument from Property Rights

Yet another defense of the classical view rests on what I shall call the argument from property rights. Who owns the corporation? The standard answer is that the shareholders do. If the shareholders own the corporation, who should decide to what end the company's profits should be used? Again, the standard answer is that the shareholder should decide. In other words, people have a right to decide how they shall invest their own resources. When you add this property right claim to the empirical thesis that shareholders want corporations to maximize profits, the complete justification is on hand. People have a right to decide how to use their property; the corporation is the property of the stockholders, and the stockholders want the corporation to maximize its profits. Since the stockholders have a right to use their property (the corporation) this way, the managers ought to seek to maximize profits. Or so the argument goes.

New Theories of the Function of the Corporation

Critique of the Utilitarian Justification of the Classical Theory

Critics of the classical view appeal to the other great tradition in ethics— the deontological tradition—as a starting point for their arguments. They remind us that corporations are chartered as a result of a kind of contract made with society; indeed a charter is a contract. Now the original contract is made on the basis that the activities of the corporation will lead to the greatest public good. The specific content of the contract, which is seldom explicit in the charter of incorporation but which has been provided by judicial interpretation and political custom, acknowledges that the *accepted* means for achieving the public good is to allow the corporation to maximize profits. However, as we have seen, the judicial interpretations and political customs rest on empirical assumptions about human nature and the nature of the competitive process. If those empirical assumptions turn out to be false, the argument for the classical view collapses. There is no further warrant in the contract for arguing that the function of a corporation is to maximize profits. The classical position stands or falls with the empirical assumptions.

However, it is just these empirical assumptions that are coming under scrutiny. Although few doubt the prominence of self-interest in human motivation, the notion of the invisible hand is particularly vulnerable to attack. The competitive process by itself is not sufficient to yield the greatest good for the greatest number. Cooperation is a necessary complement. Indeed, Adam Smith's recognition that the competitive process must be governed by rules enforced by political authority provides the starting point for our analysis. Rule-governed behavior is cooperative behavior. It requires that we agree to constrain our self-seeking activities in accordance with the rules. Surely the English philosopher Thomas Hobbes (1588–1679) is right when he argues that, in an egoistic world, some rules are required if chaos is to be avoided. In a completely egoistic world without any rules, a state of nature would exist that would be characterized by a war of all against all. In such a world an individual's life would be "nasty, brutish, and short."

The necessity of cooperative behavior can be further illustrated by applying game theory to a competitive sales office situation. Suppose that in a sales division of twenty word is received that, if overall performance of the sales unit continues to be high, an additional attractive management position will be added to the unit. Suppose that all twenty salespersons desire the new position and hence enter into competition for it. Let us suppose further that the current high performance of the sales department depends on the ability to discover new customers for one another, for example, one sales representative will always tell another about a prospective client in the other's neighborhood. Now that competition has begun for the new position, the sales representatives try to lure customers away from one another. Each salesperson would now try to gain any client for his or her account, even if that prospective client were a neighbor or friend of another in the unit. Since this salesperson is neither a neighbor nor a friend, he or she is less likely to obtain the account. Such a strategy when viewed as a unit is self-defeating; the requisite condition that overall performance of the sales unit remain high will not be met.

On the other hand, with such a competitive situation for the management position in effect, it would not be in the interest of any one salesperson to avoid trying to lure customer accounts from the other. He or she would certainly lose out on the competition for the new management position. What is needed, of course, is a binding rule of cooperation that says that each salesperson must give prospective clients to neighbors or friends of other sales representatives in the unit. Only if this rule is adopted will the end result that everyone wants—namely, the new management position—be attainable. Utilitarian results are not brought about simply by the existence of the invisible hand. The rules that govern the competitive process are equally important. If the rules are insufficient in number, inadequate in content, or not enforced, the public good will not be achieved. The traditional business view has overemphasized the benefits of competition and has underemphasized the benefits of cooperative rules. Much more will be said about the strengths and weaknesses of competition in Chapter 4.

Second, there are many goods and services that cannot be produced in sufficiently desired amounts through the competitive market process. For the market to work efficiently, one must presume that people express their true preferences in bidding for scarce goods and resources. This assumption works well enough for any commodity where my consumption precludes your consumption. Since you cannot eat the orange I have eaten, you will express your true preference for the orange and outbid me if you can. But consider a well-paved highway where my travel does not preclude yours. When it is time for highway repairs, it is in my self-interest to understate the worth of the highway to me. After all, I will still retain all my benefits if I can get other highway users to pay more. Of course, each highway user reasons as I do, and as a result the amount of money forthcoming for highway repairs is not equal to the collective desire of the community for well-paved highways. In this case, as in the case of other goods and services that resemble highways, the invisible hand of market competition cannot produce the public good.

Third, there are many by-products of business (called external diseconomies) that represent a cost borne by society although the cost was produced by business activity itself. Air and water pollution, excessive noise, and unattractive factories are some common examples. Unless these costs of doing business are taken into account, one gets a distortedly optimistic picture of the benefits of the competitive business enterprise. Moreover, it seems only fair that the cost of these by-products should be borne by the business itself. After all, if it is inappropriate for a society to subsidize a steel firm's purchase of coal, would it not also be inappropriate for society to subsidize the cost of a steel company's pollution? Unfortunately, even if a steel company would agree to pay the cost of its pollution, it is hard to see how on market grounds the costs could be assessed. Pollution is a product more like highways than like oranges. However, in this case those harmed by pollution would try to overstate their harm, and hence the company would be penalized. Methods for determining and assessing the true costs of external diseconomies currently occupies the attention of many professional economists. As of this writing, however, there is no universally accepted solution to the problem.

Fourth, a large part of American corporate activity is not competitive—at least not competitive in the sense that Adam Smith and classical economists had in mind. For some products, like telephone and utility services, it is technically not feasible for competition to exist. In other industries (e.g., automobile production), start-up costs for any potential firm are so prohibitive that competition is effectively stifled. Of course there is competition in the automobile industry, but not competition of the type you find among "mom and pop" grocery stores. Moreover, as industries have grown, society is no longer able to allow the competitive process to work. Some companies, like some cities, cannot be allowed to go bankrupt, and hence society bails them out.

These four considerations lead us to doubt that the invisible hand that governs the competitive process is sufficient to produce utilitarian results. However, even beyond these considerations, critics of the classical definition of the function of a business enterprise challenge the view that the invisible hand of competition ever could justify a utilitarian maximization. After all, the stockholders are just one constituency of a business. They are no more necessary to its success than are employees, managers, or customers. Would it not seem more likely that utilitarian results are achieved when the firm attempts to maximize the interests of all its constituencies? In Chapter 1 we distinguished the stockholder model from the stakeholder model. In the stakeholder model, the interests of all the constituencies of the firm are to be taken into account. A similar model discussed by Clarence Walton has been referred to as *household model*.[3]

A Refutation of the Property Argument

Critics of the classical theory of the function of the corporation adopt a similar strategy in attacking the right to private property argument; they criticize the empirical hypotheses on which the argument is based. In addition, they have a moral argument of their own.

While it is probably true that business practice in capitalist countries would be virtually unrecognized as business unless there were private property, many defenders of capitalism read far too much into the private property rule.

Let us distinguish among

---

[3] For an extended discussion of this model, see Clarence C. Walton, *Corporate Social Responsibilities* (Belmont, Calif.: Wadsworth Publishing Co., Inc., 1968), pp. 129–132.

1. Business should be privately owned and operated.
2. Business decisions should usually be private rather than public.
3. Businesspersons may do what they want with their property.

Whereas points 1 and 2 are generally viewed as morally acceptable rules of business practice, rule 3 is the one that is under moral challenge.

Moreover, there is no absolute right to do with one's property what one pleases. If I am selling my property, I cannot refuse to sell to a black. If I live in a development, I cannot own pigs or horses. If I own a swimming pool, it must be surrounded by a six-foot fence. If I own a pet rattlesnake, I cannot simply let it go when I grow tired of it. Property rights are always limited rights.

Most stockholders in a firm are not property owners in the way in which most single-family homeowners are. Most homeowners do not own homes simply to maximize a real estate investment. Such a homeowner lives in a home, manages it, and provides for its upkeep. Often improvements are made in the home that any competent real estate agent would agree would not return the investment if the house were sold. Indeed, this type of homeowner usually develops an attachment to the home. A house takes on a special meaning (a house is not a home). Frequently, this homeowner will not sell the home even when it is financially advantageous to do so. I know of people who have not sold their home for an astronomical profit and despite the fact that it is literally surrounded by fast-food outlets. They wish to die in the home that has been such a part of their lives all these years. This attitude is in sharp contrast to most stockholders who are indifferent absentee owners who will sell their stock whenever the price is right. Hence, all property owning does not share the same characteristics.

Having established that property ownership is not an exclusive right and that property ownership comes in many forms, one can ask which types of property ownership should have the most constraints placed upon it. Surely a good case can be made for saying that the most constraints should be on property that is held simply as a financial investment. Since the owner of such property has less incentive to take the same personal interest in managing, maintaining, and improving that corporate property as is taken in his or her personal property, there is a greater case for the constraining of corporate property rights in the interests of society.

One of the great issues in political philosophy is setting the criteria whereby my right to own and use my property must yield to the legitimate rights of others. The angry debates about smoking provide an excellent illustration. In the business context, one of the most controversial issues concerns corporate moves from one city to another or corporate closings. Should private property rights enable a corporation to move or shut down without consulting affected persons, or should the property rights of corporations be circumscribed in those respects? Consider the Olin Corporation case.

_____ Olin Corporation _____

Saltville is a small community of 2,500 located in rural southwest Virginia. Since 1892 it had been the epitome of the one-company town. By 1954, the original Mathieson Alkali Works had been taken over by the giant Olin Corporation. Although some of the symbols of the one-company town—for example, company houses and a company store—had become a thing of the past, the Olin Company was the foundation of Saltville's economic and psychological support.

In 1960, Olin Corporation's Saltville facilities employed about 1,500 people. By 1970, that employment figure had dwindled to about 800. In 1970, Olin Corporation announced that it would close its soda ash facilities in Saltville. The closing would occur in a phaseout over a two-and-one-half-year period. Presumably, a phaseout rather than an abrupt shutdown would give Olin's Saltville employees an opportunity to find other work.

In making its announcement, the company contended that three economic factors had led to its decision: (1) the failure of a 1968 modernization program of Olin's Saltville facilities to raise production, (2) the resulting rise in production costs as a result of the failure, and (3) stricter requirements by the Virginia Water Control Board that would require a $2 million expenditure at the Saltville facilities. Company officials placed most of the emphasis on the economic impact of the Virginia Water Control Board's decision.

Some were unconvinced that revised water pollution standards were the chief reason for the closing. In addition to the failure of the modernization program, the parent company had made a major error in the timing of its investment in aluminum production. Others focused on environmental issues. One study showed that Olin's Saltville facilities caused $2 million in damages per year to the river. Olin was in effect being asked to make total expenditures for pollution reduction equipment, which were equal to the damage it caused in one year. In any case, Olin never appealed the board's decision, and the state granted Olin a two-and-one-half-year exemption so that the shutdown of the Saltville facilities might be orderly.

The assumption that most people would not be out of work until mid-1972 was shattered in June 1971. It was announced that the soda ash facilities would close permanently July 1, 1971. Worsening economic factors represented by an inventory buildup were given as the cause. On November 18, 1971, Olin announced it would close its Saltville caustic soda plant on March 1, 1972. Increasing production costs and needed modernization costs were given as the reasons. The final blow fell when the Navy failed to renew a contract with an Olin Saltville hydrazine plant. Instead, the contract was given to another Olin company facility in Louisiana. Again, economic factors were cited. On June 30, 1972, all Olin facilities in Saltville were closed.

Despite the economic motivation for the closedowns, Olin took several steps to mitigate the charge that Saltville had been heartlessly sacrificed on the altar of profits. A generous severance plan and early retirement plan were implemented. Olin established a relocation assistance service. Olin donated plant, property, and equipment to Saltville and contributed $600,000 to compensate for lost taxes and for planning and development. Some were unimpressed with Olin's generosity. The company "gifts" represented huge tax write-offs, and in any case did not fully compensate Saltville for the harms it suffered.[4]

We shall not attempt to decide whether Olin's decisions were morally acceptable. Such a discussion requires a determination of the moral obligations of all corporations (Chapter 3) and an analysis of the notion of procedural justice (Chapter 3). Our discussion has shown, however, that corporate owners are neither morally nor legally permitted to do what they please with the corporate property.

The Contract Notion

If these criticisms of the empirical and conceptual foundations of the classical view of the function of the corporation are successful, some other more adequate definition of the function of the corporation will have to be found. The notion of the function of the corporation will have to be expanded. But how far? To answer this question, we must consider the so-called social contract that exists between business and society. Proponents of an expanded notion of corporate responsibility remember that a corporation exists only at the behest of society. If society becomes disenchanted with corporations, society has the power to abolish them. Two writers have put this idea in the form of a law that they have called "The Iron Law of Corporate Responsibility." That law says that "In the long run, those who do not use power in a manner which society considers responsible will tend to lose it."[5]

The first argument for an expanded definition of the function of a corporation is an argument from enlightened self-interest. The central thesis of the argument is that, if business does not expand its notion of corporate responsibility beyond maximizing profits, society through government will intervene, and the end result will be that business will suffer. It is better business if business cleans up its own house rather than if the government does it. Government regulations and controls are the real enemy. If additional regulations and controls are to be avoided, then business must take on added responsibilities on its own accord. Persons familiar with the literature in corporate responsibility will recognize that

---

[4] This case is taken from Thomas L. Beauchamp and Norman E. Bowie, eds., *Ethical Theory and Business*, (Englewood Cliffs, N.J.: Prentice-Hall, Inc., 1979), p. 123.

[5] Keith Davis and Robert L. Blomstrom, *Business and Society: Environment and Responsibility*, 3rd ed. (New York: McGraw-Hill Book Company, 1975), p. 50.

this argument from enlightened self-interest is by far the most common one. Many corporate leaders believe that increased social responsibility is in the long-run best interests of the corporation.

However, the iron law of corporate responsibility is not a moral law. Just because society has the power to force corporations to increase their social responsibilities does not mean that society is right in making that demand. Indeed, those favoring the classical definition could argue that society's demands are immoral. After all, a promise is a promise, a contract is a contract. All sides agree that originally the contract relationship was interpreted so that business's main responsibility was to make profits. Now society wants to change the rules of the game. Government officials in particular impose new requirements on business, and each change in the political wind brings a swirl of new regulations. Since business activity does depend heavily on the notion of contract, one must realize that contracts must remain stable through time. If the terms of the contract are constantly changing, then you really do not have a contract any more. And, without the stability of contracts, business itself becomes impossible.

What often motivates demand for changes in the terms of a contract is the pressure of those who have lost something or are in some way made worse off as a result of the contract. After all, if someone buys stock in AT&T and the price of AT&T then falls unexpectedly, the person who bought the stock is worse off. The fact that the person is worse off does not give him or her the right to renege on the contract. Circumstances do change and people are made worse off as a result of contracts they have made. This should come as no surprise. Long before we enter the world of business we make promises, and sometimes keeping our promises does work to our disadvantage. However, we still ought to keep our promises. Now since a contract is a type of promise, why shouldn't society keep its contracts?

This response by proponents of the classical definition of a corporation's responsibilities raises a number of difficult and complex issues. At the outset, however, one would have to agree that the proponents have a point. Promises and contracts do impose duties of compliance, and the fact that keeping a promise or a contract is not always beneficial is frequently irrelevant. One is still obligated to keep the contract.

Perhaps the best way to respond to proponents of the classical view is to consider the more generic notion of promise keeping. Usually we do have a duty to keep our promises, even when keeping them works out to our disadvantage. Usually—but not always. Promises can be overridden. For example, if an angry jealous husband demands that I keep my promise to return his gun, morality requires that I break my promise if I think he will use the gun to kill his wife. Countless other examples can easily be constructed. The underlying principle is that one can violate one's duty to keep a promise on the basis of some higher or overriding moral obligation, for example, saving a human life. It is important to note that the breaking of the promise must be made on *moral* grounds; it cannot be done on the basis of convenience or mere self-interest. Hence, to effectively respond to proponents of the classical view, one must argue that the demands of society to rewrite the social contract with business are made on the basis of moral obligations that override the contract itself.

The first place to turn is to the contract itself. The simple existence of a written agreement does not automatically give rise to a valid contract any more than an uttering of the words "I promise" gives rise to a legitimate promise. If someone twists my arm and threatens to break it unless I give him $5, the arm twister cannot later argue that I have a duty on the basis of my promise to give him $5. In the underworld a "contract" to carry out a "hit" on a person is not a legitimate contract. The mob leader has no moral right to complain if the contract is not carried out.

What are the conditions for a legitimate contract? A systematic, universally accepted answer to this question is not readily available. Our discussion will be limited to some rather widely proposed conditions. First, the contract must not be made under duress. Surely the classical interpretation of the contract between business and society was not made under duress. The interpretation was encouraged by the representatives of society in government and enforced in courts of law. Second, all parties affected by the contract must be parties to it. As to whether or not the classical interpretation meets this condition, there will certainly be debate. Since our society is a representative democracy, it can be argued that all Americans through their representatives did endorse the contract as classically interpreted. On the other hand, even those who agree that democracy is the best form of government admit that it has imperfections. This was especially true when the terms of the original contract were formulated. In the earliest years blacks and women could not vote, and only within the last generation has the franchise been a practical reality for blacks. There are many arguments to show that representative democracy has not adequately represented the poor. Indeed, these kinds of criticism could be developed into a Marxian theoretical framework that argues that the original interpretation of society's contract with business was imposed on the proleteriat by a minority bourgeoise. Without assessing the validity of the Marxist critique, suffice it to say that many who are poor, or female, or members of minority groups do not believe that their ancestors were represented adequately as the classical interpretation of the contract with society evolved.

Third, the decline of *caveat emptor* (let the buyer beware) and the rise of consumer legislation illustrates another condition for valid contracts. Parties to the contract must possess a certain minimum level of intelligence. Society through government has a responsibility to protect ignorant people from making contracts that are clearly not in their interest. Just how wide the responsibility should be is a matter of great debate. Some people believe that it is morally inappropriate and causally impossible for the goverment to protect people from failure and loss. However, nearly everyone agrees that some contracts have been unfair to the ignorant poor. Just how extensive government regulation should be in this area is a discussion for Chapter 5.

It does seem evident, however, that the parties who accepted the classical interpretation of the contract between business and society did not run afoul of the ignorance condition. The parties to the classical interpretation of the function of business had little in common with ignorant consumers.

Comments about ignorance are not completely irrelevant, however. When put into practice, the view that the corporation has as its function the increasing of profits has had some unforeseen and undesirable consequences. The pollution of our air and water, noise, the ugliness of factories, as well as shortcuts on safety and product quality are all examples of such unforeseen and undesirable consequences. Other persons would cite planned obsolescence, the growth of advertising, and the alleged undesirable effects of corporate life on the individual personality and family structure as additional consequences. In its broadest form, some critics hold the world of business responsible for most of America's social problems. The behavior of the corporation is allegedly harmful behavior. Should that charge prove to be partially correct, even if the corporations were ignorant of the harmful effects, we may have a moral basis for arguing that the classical definition of the contract that business has with society should be changed.

Fourth, the contract itself must be of a moral nature. Since the classical interpretation of the contract maintains that it is the legitimate function of business to pursue profits, the contract permits business to have an important effect on how scarce goods and resources are to be distributed. Opponents of the classical contract interpretation could argue that the terms of the contract violate canons of distributive justice. After all, the profits of a corporation do not accrue to the corporation; they belong to flesh and blood persons called shareholders. When one increases, or on the extreme *maximizes*, profits, one is increasing the return to shareholders. A corporation could distribute excess revenue in other ways. It could increase the wages of its employees, or lower the prices of its products, or even put more into research and development. Indeed if one adopts the not unreasonable assumption that most large stockholders are wealthier than are most assembly-line employees, one could argue that it is more just to raise wages or lower prices than to maximize profits. As we have seen, Henry Ford took precisely this position. He was sued and in court he lost. Moreover, in its decision the court recognized the distributive impact of various management decisions but declared that a corporation was not a charitable organization. But is such a view just?

Those who support the classical definition of the function of the corporation respond to this criticism as follows: A society should be concerned with minimum standards of living. However, ensuring a minimum standard of living is the proper function of government; it is not the job of the corporation. So long as the corporation and those individuals who have succeeded in the market pay their taxes to support provisions for adequate living standards for all, both the corporation and its managers have done all that is morally required.

Can society demand that the social contract with business be rewritten because the original contract violated the moral requirements for contract making? The evidence is ambiguous, and hence I do not believe the argument can be made sufficiently convincing. Better arguments are at hand. The key to one of these arguments is found in our discussion of the ignorance condition. Society was ignorant of what economists call the external diseconomies of the private economy. These external diseconomies were hidden costs that have been imposed (without compensation) on society. In other words the original contract with business that encourages maximization of shareholder profits imposes significant harm on society—harm that no reasonable person could have foreseen. Let us consider this argument in some detail.

The Avoidable Harm Interpretation Another way of determining whether or not a business contract is of a moral nature is to determine whether or not the contract violates what some writers in moral philosophy refer to as the moral minimum. A person's behavior is consistent with the moral minimum if it causes no avoidable harm to others. The notion of the moral minimum should be contrasted with what might be called the moral ideal where one acts to produce the greatest good (the injunction of traditional utilitarianism). Many moral philosophers consider the utilitarian moral ideal too stringent. We need not always so act as to produce the greatest good. However, we should all subscribe to the moral minimum. A corporation morally need not surrender profits to produce the greatest social good. However, it is morally required to surrender profits when corporate behavior violates the moral minimum (inflicts avoidable harm on others). On this basis, the classical contract with society might be rewritten so that it would read, "The function of a corporation is to maximize profits so long as profit making does not cause avoidable harm."

But what counts as an avoidable harm? It is worth quoting some representative exponents of this view at length.

> *Although the notion of social injury is imprecise and although many hard cases will be encountered in applying it, we think that it is a helpful designa-*

tion and that cases can be decided on the basis of it. In the law, many notions (such as negligence in the law of torts or consideration in the law of contracts) are equally vague but have received content from repeated decision-making over time. We would hope that under our proposed Guidelines similar "case law" would develop. Moreover, our Guidelines attempt to give some content to the notion of social injury by referring to external norms: social injury is defined as "particularly including activities which violate, or frustrate the enforcement of, rules of domestic or international law intended to protect individuals against deprivation of health, safety or basic freedoms."

In sum, we would affirm the prima facie obligation of all citizens, both individual and institutional, to avoid and correct self-caused social injury. Much more in the way of affirmative acts may be expected of certain kinds of citizens, but none is exempt from this "moral minimum."[6]

Unfortunately, this definition falls short of the work it must do. Proponents of the classical view will surely object that our condition is too strong. For example, we know statistically that about 50,000 persons per year will die and that nearly 250,000 will be seriously injured in automobile accidents. Such death and injury is avoidable. Does not our avoidable harm criterion require that the production of automobiles for profit cease?

Surely some refinement of the avoidable harm condition is required. Society does accept many types of avoidable harm. We take certain risks—ride in planes, have bridges built, and mine coal—to pursue certain goals. So long as the risks are known, it is not wrong that some avoidable harm be permitted so that other social and individual goals can be achieved. The avoidable harm criterion needs revision.

Using the automobile as a paradigm, let us consider the necessary refinements. It is a fundamental principle of ethics that "ought" implies "can." That expression means that you can only be held morally responsible for events that are within your power. In the "ought implies can" principle, the overwhelming majority of highway deaths and injuries is not the responsibility of the auto manufacturer. Only those deaths and injuries attributable to unsafe automobile design can be attributed to them.

The "ought implies can" principle can also be used to absolve the auto companies for responsibility for death and injury from safety defects that the company could not reasonably know existed; the company could not be expected to do anything about them.

But even on these refinements, can we not say that the company has an obligation to build a car as safe as it knows how? No. The standards

[6] John C. Simon, Charles W. Powers, and Jon P. Gunnemann, *The Ethical Investor: Universities and Corporate Responsibility* (New Haven, Conn.: Yale University Press, 1972), p. 21.

for safety must be within one's capability ("ought implies can" again). Comments about engineering and equipment capability are obvious enough. But for a business, "capability" is also a function of profitability. A company that builds a maximally safe car at a cost that puts it at a competitive disadvantage and hence threatens its survival is building a safe car that lies beyond the *capability* of the company.

Now critics of the automobile industry will express horror at these remarks, since by making capability a function of profitability society will continue to have avoidable deaths and injuries. However, the situation is not as dire as the critics imagine. Certainly, capability should not be sacrificed completely so that profits can be maximized. The decision to build products that are cheaper in cost but are not maximally safe is a social decision that has widespread support. The arguments occur over the line between safety and cost. What we have is a classical trade-off situation. What is desired is some approximate mix between engineering safety and reasonable profits. To say that there must be some mix between engineering safety and reasonable profits is not to justify all the decisions made by the automobile companies. Ford Motor Company did make a morally inappropriate choice in placing Pinto gas tanks where it did. What is to be emphasized is that questions of safety involve questions of value. What risks is society willing to undertake?

Given the indeterminancy of the phrase "avoidable harm," I propose to define the moral minimum in a somewhat different way. In Chapter 3, I will ask what universal moral norms must be generally adhered to if social institutions, including businesses, are to exist. I will argue that most of these norms are rules of fair play, which, following Rawls, I call the rules of justice. Hence, my first revision of the classical definition of the function of the corporation is as follows: The function of a corporation is to maximize profits consistent with the universal moral norms of justice (fair play).

The Violation of Rights Interpretation There is yet a third way of assessing the current contract between business and society. Does the contract violate any legitimate rights of either the parties to the contract or of those affected by it? This issue was introduced in Chapter 1. It seemed to us that employers often insisted on a kind of loyalty that may violate individual rights. As an introduction to this issue, consider the following business practices.

For many years corporations frequently moved upwardly mobile executives from one region of the country to another. They also insisted on long hours and other indications of "devotion" to the company. Even now, many business firms insist on certain dress codes that are allegedly consistent with the "image" of the industry. Some companies insist that employees not belong to "controversial" organizations or engage in "controversial" activities. I have been told that one large well-known company instructs its employees to avoid certain bars and other entertainment spots in the city where one of the company's plants is located. I have also been told that another large well-known company makes a certain level of contribution to the United Fund virtually mandatory. All these activities raise serious questions about violations of individual rights.

The language of individuals' rights is relatively new in the vocabulary of the corporation. Since most corporations are organized hierarchically, there is a long tradition of orders flowing from top down to the bottom. The most pervasive character trait of a good employee is loyalty—willingness to sacrifice—and evidence of team spirit. Even today, in articles in the prestigious *Harvard Business Review*, managers praise the virtues of loyalty and decry its decline. In the language of Chapter 1, one might say that the primary duty cutting across all stations is the duty of loyalty. For many, it is the chief virtue for any employee.

To argue that business must honor individual rights is to present an unfamiliar demand upon the behavior of many businesses. In the next chapter, the arguments that business ought to honor individual rights will be developed at some length. For the present I will simply assert that contracts for profit making that are in violation of the legitimate rights of individuals are in violation of the criterion that legitimate contracts must be of a moral nature. My final revision of the classical definition of the corporation is as follows: The function of a corporation is to maximize profits consistent with the universal moral norms of justice and with respect for legitimate individual rights. I shall refer to this revised definition as the neoclassical definition of the function of the corporation.

By revising the classical definition, a lot of work has been postponed until chapter 3. Before turning to these tasks, however, we must consider redefinitions of the function of the corporation that are considerably broader than the neoclassical definition outlined here.

The Maximal Account of Corporate Responsibility

The neoclassical definition of the purpose of a corporation added certain moral constraints to the classical maximization of profits view so that the pursuit of profit might be morally acceptable. However, many, including many within the business community, would argue for an even broader notion of corporate responsibility. All, however, agree that the pursuit of profit is one of the essential goals of business.

Perhaps one of the best known articles arguing for the broader view is Keith Davis's "Five Propositions for Social Responsibility."[7] Two of

---

[7] Keith Davis, "Five Propositions for Social Responsibility," *Business Horizons*, Vol. 18 (June 1975), 19–24.

Davis's propositions refer to taking the true costs of business activity into account. Since this topic has already been discussed in providing the neoclassical definition of the function of a business, we will only discuss the remaining three propositions.

The first of the remaining propositions contends that "social responsibility arises from social power." Since business has tremendous social power, it has very extensive social responsibilities as well. In all business decisions, the overall interests of society must be taken into account. Under a second proposition business has a responsibility to be fully open about its operations. What is often referred to as a policy of "open disclosure" should be voluntarily adopted by business. For example, such open disclosure would be useful for encouraging widespread public discussion when a firm is contemplating closing down a factory or when it wishes to introduce a highly beneficial drug that unfortunately contains side effects. The final proposition contends that business institutions have responsibilities for social involvement in areas of their competence where major social needs exist. A commitment to this last proposition is a rather open-ended commitment to social responsibility. What arguments can be given on its behalf? Perhaps the most common is what may be called the argument from citizenship. Corporations are institutional members of society. Now surely, if the individual members of society have an obligation to improve society—to leave the world better than we found it—certainly corporations do. After all, corporations, unlike individuals, were created by society. Corporations are citizens, and citizens have civic duties and responsibilities.

A second closely related argument is based on the duty of gratitude. Corporations benefit from society. On the basis of the commonly accepted principle that one owes debts of gratitude toward those who benefit us, the corporation has certain debts that it owes to society.

The final argument is provided by Davis's first proposition—namely, that social responsibility arises from social power. Great power is a gift, and it should be used to good ends. American business has thrived in this representative democracy and as a result has tremendous resources at its disposal. These resources should be used wisely to assist in solving social ills.

Before assessing these arguments, let us consider another way of determining the full breadth of corporate responsibilities. Clarence Walton has developed a number of models of business that range from some that resemble the classical model to others that incorporate a broad degree of social involvement.[8] The profit maximization view can be divided in two, depending on whether the emphasis is on short-run or long-run profits. Walton gives the short-run profit view the name "austere

---

[8] Walton, *Corporate Social Responsibilities*, pp. 127–141.

model." Concern for long-run profits is captured by what Walton calls the "investment model." The investment model is captured by the court decision in *A.P. Smith Manufacturing Company* v. *Barlow*, which ruled that corporate decisions concerning such things as charity are legitimate when they enhance long-run profits.

The household model compares business with a large family. In this model, it is the employees rather than the stockholders who are the chief responsibility of the corporation. The household model accepts as its first proposition the fact that human resources are a firm's most precious asset; consequently, anything that depersonalizes the employee or assigns the employee a low rating in the corporation's list of priorities is to be rejected as unsound.[9] In the classical view, a worker is simply a factor of production no different from capital, machinery, or raw materials. Employees are to be combined with the factors of production in the most efficient manner. Such a view is totally rejected by adherents to the household model. Whereas in the classical model ultimate concern is with profits for shareholders, in the household model ultimate concern is for the welfare of the employees.

The analysis provided by Keith Davis would be incorporated into the civic model. As expressed by Walton, "Citizenship . . . is not limited simply to a discharge of formally imposed obligations any more than citizenship for the individual is fully met by paying taxes or by voting. The civic model envisages a positive business commitment to the political system of democracy."[10]

Walton considers a final model that, should it become increasingly adopted, would revolutionize business practice. He refers to it as the artistic model. In this model, business is characterized chiefly as a creative enterprise. Contrary to popular stereotypes and to some practice, a business should not be hierarchical, rigid, and bureaucratic. Rather, business is the ideal social institution for providing opportunities for individual experimentation, problem solving, and the undertaking of work. Business decisions are challenging and require creative individuals.

Suggestions for expanding the functions of the corporation beyond those enumerated in the neoclassical definition do have difficulties, however. Corporations would not fit neatly into Walton's models—especially into those models that do not have the pursuit of profit as a central feature. A corporation cannot consider only the needs of the workers as the household model suggests. The civic model "envisages a positive business commitment to the political system of democracy." But what does a corporate citizen owe to America? We all have duties as citizens, but these duties are not openended. Perhaps corporations should be less

---

[9] Ibid., p. 130.
[10] Ibid., p. 137.

hierarchical; perhaps they should provide more opportunities for individual experimentation. But there are limits as to how much individualism can be tolerated. In any case, promoting creativity cannot be the chief function of the corporation. Walton's models remind us of activities that corporations should undertake, but no one of his models can serve as *the* model of the corporation. Once multiple purposes are introduced, considerations of weighing and balancing must be addressed. However, these considerations are absent from most of the literature on the topic.

The problem of open-endedness afflicts some of Davis's analyses as well. The injunction to take social responsibilities into account and to assist in solving social problems (where a corporation is competent) makes impossible demands on a corporation. At the practical level, it ignores the impact that such activities have on profit. At the theoretical level, it shares a difficulty common to utilitarianism; that is, it makes every action a moral action and hence makes the moral life too demanding.

Finally, one might consider the stakeholder theory. The term "stakeholder" was apparently coined in an internal memorandum at the Stanford Research Institute in 1963. It was defined as "those groups without whose support the organization would cease to exist." The list of stakeholders includes shareholders, employees, customers, suppliers, and lenders.[11] In that theory, the function of business is to harmonize the interests of its various constituencies. However, the stakeholder theory is similarly incomplete. A theory for harmonizing the interests of the various stakeholders is required.[12]

Summary

Let us review progress thus far. In Chapter 1, we determined that the starting point for business ethics was with one's job description—in philosophical parlance with one's station and its duties. However, we found that the job description had inherent within it conflicts of duties. Perhaps, it was suggested, we could resolve some of these conflicts if we examined the nature of the corporation itself. In this chapter we have discussed various theories of the nature of the corporation. We presented a neoclassical theory that opted for a profit maximization view constrained by justice and respect for individual rights and a broader contemporary view that might best be summarized as opting for the maximization

---

[11] Quoted from R. Edward Freeman and David L. Reed "Stockholders & Stakeholders: A New Perspective on Corporate Governance," Wharton ARC Publication No. 21681. Philadelphia, PA., January 1981, pp. 2–3.

[12] For the most advanced work aimed at providing a mechanism for harmonization, see Ibid.

and harmonization of the interests of all of a business's constituencies. It is clear that this discussion does mark progress. We can now say that any duty assigned to one's position is not legitimate if it cannot be justified on the basis of one of the acceptable theories of the function of a corporation.

Although our analysis has enabled us to improve upon the classical definition of the function of a corporation, there are at least two competing models remaining that have solid arguments in their favor: the neoclassical and maximally broad accounts of social responsibility. Problems remain, however. As yet we do not have a proof for the contention that corporations should honor individual rights. Moreover, the broad view refers to the harmonization and maximization of the corporation's constituencies, but no clue is provided for determining how this harmonization is to be done. What does the chief executive of a corporation do when interests of the workers conflict with the interests of society as a whole in decisions as to how far the corporation should go in the installation of antipollution devices?

Finally, the question as to whether job obligations consistent with an acceptable definition of the function of a corporation can be superseded by demands of a universal morality has not been addressed. This question, as well as others, will be addressed in Chapter 3, where we examine the moral precepts that underlie business practice itself.

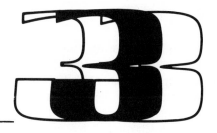

Moral Presuppositions of Business

In discussions of business ethics, it is not uncommon for several of the discussants to assume rather cynical postures: "There is no such thing as business ethics." "Business ethics is a contradiction in terms." "The business of business is business; ethics just isn't relevant." Although these remarks might be taken as representing the cynical extreme, the attitude that business must play by a different set of rules is a common one.

This chapter begins with the argument that this common perception is totally mistaken. Rather, it will be argued that, as a matter of necessity, business practice must rest on a moral base. If it did not, business practice would be impossible. In other words, it will be argued that those who take this "There is no business ethics" position are fundamentally mistaken because the very enterprise of business presupposes that the participants in business transactions must subscribe to a set of universal moral norms.

A later part of the chapter will discuss departures from these moral norms. The discussion will have two components: (1) how many departures from these norms *can* business practice tolerate and (2) how many departures from these norms *should* business practice tolerate.

The Universal Norms Presupposed by Business

In this section I will try to prove that, unless business adheres to a minimum standard of justice and gives recognition to the rights of those engaged in the practice of business, business practice is impossible. To accomplish this proof, I must first show that such practices as lying, stealing, fraud, and bribery are all universally immoral and that business practice presupposes that such actions are immoral. To accomplish this latter goal, we must consider the philosophy of one of the greatest moral philosophers, Immanuel Kant (1724–1804).

In Chapter 1, the term deontological ethics was introduced. One of the most distinguished deontologists was Immanuel Kant. He believed that the foundations of morality could not be secure unless they were grounded in something universal—something common to all men and women. In his view, the only possible candidate was human reason itself. He defended the view that an examination of reason would establish the fundamental laws of the moral life. Kant articulated three formulations of one fundamental law, which he called "The Categorical Imperative." The three formulations of the categorical imperative can be put roughly as follows:

1. One ought never to act unless one is willing to have the maxim on which one acts become a universal law.

2. Treat all humankind as ends and never as means merely.

3. Act as if you were a member of an ideal society in which you were both subject and sovereign.

Before applying these principles to business practice, a brief explanation is in order. The first formulation might be called the principle of consistency of action. To understand what Kant is driving at, one should recall that familiar moral principle—the Golden Rule: Do unto others as you would have them do unto you. Kant's moral philosophy can be viewed as an extensive reworking of the Golden Rule.

In teaching the Golden Rule, the point is to focus on how you want to be treated and then to argue that you should treat others the same way. The reason we should treat others the same way is found in the principle of consistency. In this context, it means that like cases should be treated alike. A few examples will illustrate not only the Golden Rule but also the argument underlying it.

Suppose that two teams are discussing the rules to be used for an ad hoc baseball game. The pitcher for the Red Sox argues vehemently for keeping the traditional "three strikes and you're out rule." However, upon coming to bat, that very same pitcher now argues for four strikes. Would not the pitcher be guilty of contradicting himself? Suppose that the pitcher replies that he is not contradicting himself at all. When he agreed earlier to the three-strike rule, he was the pitcher. Now that he is the batter, the four-strike rule seems more appropriate. Such a reply would never do, but why not? Would this person allow the opposing team's pitcher to change the rule? Presumably not. To make the point another way, would this person accept a rule in which a person could change the rules of the game as he took different positions in the game? Again, presumably not.

To apply the analogy to moral problems, suppose that someone were to advocate discriminatory policies against Jews. To be consistent, that person would have to advocate discrimination even if he himself should turn out to be a Jew. Presumably, he would not be willing to be treated discriminatorily, and hence, as a matter of *logical consistency,* he cannot recommend discriminatory practices against Jews. Morality is not simply a matter of treating others as you would like them to treat you. It is also a matter of not treating others in ways that you would not accept if you were they. Kant's point is that morality requires consistency of action and judgment when you are both on the receiving and giving end. Morality requires that you not make an exception of yourself, that you not engage in practices or follow rules that you could not recommend to everyone.

Kant has a worthy point. Sometimes this consistency requirement is captured by the notion of justice: Some of the clearest cases of immoral behavior involve a person's trying to make an exception of himself or herself. One should not try to push into a line of people waiting to buy tickets to a popular movie. A student should not cheat on exams. A business executive should not engage in the practices of giving kickbacks and bribes. These practices involve making exceptions of oneself or exempting oneself from the rules without being willing to grant similar privileges to others.

But suppose that one were to reply to Kant as follows: "I don't care if other people try to take advantage of the rules by making exceptions of themselves. If they can get away with it, more power to them." In the business context, such a person would be willing to participate in a business environment where deception is expected. In situations like this, the Golden Rule fails us. The answer it gives depends on how the person contemplating a given action wants to be treated himself or herself. Suppose that the way in which one wants to be treated is immoral in itself—suppose that one doesn't care if others try to deceive him or her. What would the Golden Rule say now?

Kant has a ready answer. Deceptive practices, he argues, are contradictory. They are not consistent with the larger social practices of which they are a part. Consider cheating on exams. Suppose that a student were to reflect on whether it is permissible to cheat on an exam. If the student is consistent, he must agree to allow any student to cheat. If he does not allow cheating, he is contradicting himself. In Kantian language, he would not be willing to have the maxim of his action be a universal law. On the other hand, if he is consistent and recommends cheating, then the purpose of the exam is undermined. When a large number of students cheat, the professor detects the violation and the exam is not counted. But, if the exam is not counted, no one gains from cheating.

To universalize cheating would be self-defeating. Kant's point is implicitly recognized by the business community when corporate officials despair of the immoral practices of corporations and denounce executives engaging in shady practices as undermining the business enterprise itself.

The Morality of Promise Keeping

Kant's analysis is especially germane when applied to the act of making contracts and the associated idea of promise keeping. When any deontologist enumerates the various relevant considerations that enter into determining what one ought or ought not to do, whether or not one has promised always appears on the list. Indeed, the notion of promise keeping is central to moral thought. The injunction that one ought to keep one's promises is so solidly ingrained in both moral discourse and moral practice that it may be taken as one of the basic moral phenomena. Any ethical theory that cannot give an adequate account of this bedrock principle of morality that we have an obligation to keep our promises is seriously deficient.

Kant's strategy is to show that, if one contemplated breaking a promise, the maxim for that act could not be universalized; that is, promise breaking cannot be made a universal law. If one were consistently to recommend that anyone should lie when it worked to his or her advantage, the very practice of truth telling would be undermined. The universalization of rules that allow lying would entitle everyone to lie to you, just as you could lie to them. But, in this case, one could never tell if a person were telling the truth or lying. There would be no point to making promises and hence no point to promise breaking. In this way any attempt to make promise breaking a universal law would be self-defeating.

Kant's point can be restated so that it applies specifically to business. There are many ways of making a promise. One of the more formal ways is by a contract. A contract is an agreement between two or more parties, usually enforceable by law, for the doing or not doing of some definite thing. The contract device is extremely useful in business. The hiring of employees, the use of credit, the ordering and supplying of goods, and the notion of warranty, to name but a few, all make use of the contract device. Indeed the contract is such an important part of business operation that it is often overlooked. This is a serious blunder. Using a Kantian-type argument, I maintain that, if contract breaking were universalized, then business practice would be impossible. If a participant in business were to universally advocate violating contracts, such advocacy would be self-defeating, just as the universal advocacy of lying and cheating were seen to be self-defeating.

Let us begin with a quotation from Kenneth Boulding:

> *that without an integrative framework, exchange itself cannot develop, because exchange, even in its most primitive form involves trust and credibility.*[1]

In business relations, this trust and credibility is exhibited in promise keeping, especially in the keeping of contracts.

Let us take a simple business transaction and move out to more complicated ones. In almost every case of a cash-for-product transaction, either the purchaser receives the good before paying or the purchaser pays before receiving the good. Seldom is the transfer simultaneous. What would happen to business if, in an attempt to receive something for nothing, it was common practice for the purchaser to claim that he or she had paid when he or she had not. Or suppose the salesperson claimed that the customer had not paid when he or she had paid. If such behavior were universalized, ordinary commerce would become impossible. If such behavior merely became more common, ordinary commerce would become more time consuming, more costly, and less efficient.

With the expansion of credit, cash for commodity purchases is diminishing. Credit arrangements enable the purchaser to possess the goods and services that he or she desires on the promise to pay for them later. But what if delinquencies and attempted fraud became universal? The entire institution of purchase by credit would collapse.

There is some empirical evidence concerning the breakdown of credit as delinquencies have become more common. Recently, some people have discovered that they must pay the family doctor directly rather than be billed. Upon inquiring about the reason for this new regulation, they were told that such a large number of people failed to pay their doctor bills that the doctor was forced to abandon credit. A more universal breakdown in credit would spell chaos for our market economy.

Kant's strategy was to show that, if one accepts certain practices, then certain sorts of behavior are self-defeating. Such behavior undermines the practice that has been accepted. In the preceding discussion I have shown how lying and cheating undercut the practice of making contracts, a practice essential to business. Such practices cannot be universalized and, hence, from the Kantian perspective lying and cheating by business persons is immoral.

Kant's strategy enables us to provide an answer to one of the questions we raised concerning the morality of my station and its duties, namely, "Is there a higher morality that supersedes role morality in all its forms?" We

---

[1] Kenneth E. Boulding, "The Basis of Value Judgments in Economics," in *Human Values and Economic Policy*, ed. Sidney Hook (New York: New York University Press, 1967), p. 68.

now see that the answer to that question is surely yes. To accept the practice of business, one must also accept the universal moral obligations that business presupposes. It would then follow that no role (station) within business could have as one of its requirements an obligation that went contrary to these universal moral rules. Such a role-related obligation would be self-defeating. Duties required by role morality would always be superseded by the moral requirements whenever these requirements were presupposed by the practice of business and the role-related obligations were inconsistent with them.

This argument, which establishes that promise keeping is a necessary aspect of business ethics, can be generalized to show that business practice requires the adoption of a minimum standard of justice. If my general argument succeeds, support will be provided for the neoclassical definition of the function of the corporation explicated in Chapter 2. I take as my point of departure the account of justice developed by the contemporary philosopher John Rawls who has articulated the view that justice is best understood as fairness.

Consider an individual who voluntarily participates in a social institution and thereby accepts its rules and regulations. Presumably, these rules work out to the long-run benefit of those participating in the institution or at least are likely to do so. Otherwise, the person would not voluntarily participate in the institution. However, one who accepts the benefits of an institution, including the benefits derived when others participating in the institution follow the rules and regulations, but who himself or herself does not play by the rules, is unfair. He or she is a free loader—one who accepts the benefits without paying any of the costs.

> in everyday life an individual, if he is so inclined, can sometimes win even greater benefits for himself by taking advantage of the cooperative efforts of others. Sufficiently many persons may be doing their share so that when special circumstances allow him not to contribute (perhaps his omission will not be found out), he gets the best of both worlds. . . . We cannot preserve a sense of justice and all that this implies while at the same time holding ourselves ready to act unjustly should doing so promise some personal advantage.[2]

This kind of analysis has direct application to the practice of business. Consider what Rawls says about contracts:

> Such ventures are often hard to initiate and to maintain. This is especially evident in the case of covenants, that is, in those instances where one person is to perform before the other. For this person may believe that the second party will not do his part, and therefore the scheme never gets going. . . . Now in these situations there may be no way of assuring the party who is to perform first except by giving him a promise, that is, by putting oneself under an obligation to carry through later. Only in this way can the

---

[2] John Rawls, *A Theory of Justice* (Cambridge, Mass.: Harvard University Press, 1971), pp. 497, 569.

scheme be made secure so that both can gain from the benefits of their cooperation.[3]

As we have seen, the making of contracts is essential to business practice. The keeping of contracts is one of the rules and regulations of business practice. Persons participating in business activity benefit from that rule. To fail to keep one's contracts while participating in business is unfair and hence unjust. One is benefiting from the rules that others adhere to without adhering to them oneself.

A similar analysis can be given for such activities as theft, fraud, the use of kickbacks, and bribery. All such acts are acts of deception. If universalized, such activities would undermine the practice of business as surely as would the universalizing of contract breaking. This point is certainly accepted by the Better Business Bureau, an agency that is guided by the view that deceptive business practices undercut confidence in business. Hence, theft, fraud, kickbacks, and bribes are unacceptable business practices. From the Kantian perspective, such acts are immoral since they cannot be universalized. Hence, such acts join the breaking of contracts as immoral business practices. Prohibitions against these acts are fundamental moral norms essential to business practice.

A person who participates in business practice and engages in the practice of giving bribes or kickbacks is behaving unjustly. Such a person is receiving the benefits of the rules against such activities without supporting the rules personally. It is just such "free loading" that Rawls characterizes as unfair or unjust. Moreover, if such unfairness were practiced by everyone (made universal), business practice would be impossible. With respect to any kind of cooperative human activity, including business, the universalization of "free loading" would be self-defeating. In this way we can establish that justice is a universal norm presupposed by business practice.

The conclusion that justice is a universal norm presupposed by business practice fits nicely with the neoclassical definition of the function of a corporation. Another form of Kantian argument will establish another characteristic of the neoclassical definition of the function of the corporation, specifically the characteristic that a corporation must not, as it pursues profit, deny legitimate individual rights.

Business and Individual Rights

To develop this argument, the focus is on the second formulation of the categorical imperative—that formulation that can be referred to as the principle of respect for persons. Since the principle is often overlooked or is violated in business practice, it is important to argue for its centrality at some length.

---

[3] Ibid., p. 347.

Kant, in the tradition of Aristotle, recognizes that only human beings are capable of being motivated by the moral rules laid down by the categorical imperative. It is human beings that place values on other things; these other things have conditional value because they only acquire this value as the result of human action. Human beings, on the other hand, have unconditioned value, that is, value apart from any special circumstances that confer value. Since all human beings and only human beings have this unconditional value, it is always inappropriate to use another human being merely as a means to some end—as if they had instrumental value only. Hence, Kant argues, one should always treat a human being or a person with unconditional value as an end and never teat a human being merely as a means toward your own ends. The reasoning used to establish the first formulation of the categorical imperative is appropriate here. Each person looks upon himself or herself as possessing unconditioned value. If one is to avoid inconsistency, one must view all other human beings as possessors of unconditioned value as well.

Kant's principle of respect for persons can be applied directly to business practice. A Kantian would take strong exception to the view that employees are to be treated like mere equipment in the production process. Human labor should never be treated like machinery, industrial plants, and capital, solely in accordance with economic laws for profit maximization. Any economic system that fails to recognize this distinction between human beings and other nonhuman factors of production is morally deficient. In this way, Kantian ethical theory provides a criticism of the classical theory of the nature of the corporation. In the classical view, human labor is treated exactly like the other nonhuman factors of production, and hence that view is subject to Kant's criticism.[4]

Kant's second formulation of the categorical imperative has another application when applied to that essential business practice of contract making. We can use the contract notion to establish the central thesis that business firms must admit that employees have certain rights that must be respected. The structure of the argument is as follows:

1. One person can enter a valid business contract only if the parties to the contract are responsible autonomous adults.

2. If a person is a responsible autonomous adult, then that person must view himself or herself and be viewed by others as a moral agent.

3. One can be a moral agent only if one has rights that he or she can press as claims against others.

---

[4] For a statement of the classical position, see F. A. Hayek "The Corporation in a Democratic Society," in *Management and Corporations, 1985*, eds. Melvin Anshen and George Bach (New York: McGraw-Hill Book Company, 1960), pp. 102–104.

4. Therefore, a person who enters a valid business contract is a person who has rights.

5. To recognize that one has rights is to recognize that other persons entering the business contract have rights as well.

6. Therefore, a person entering a valid business contract must recognize the rights claims of the other contractees.

Premise 1 asks who are the promisers and promisees. They are persons who must be considered to be responsible autonomous agents. In other words, such persons are free adults who can be held accountable for their actions. Generally speaking, contracts with children, mental defectives, and criminals are not binding. The ideal contract maker is a responsible autonomous adult.

Premise 2 exploits the conceptual relationship between being an autonomous responsible individual and being a moral individual. In considering yourself as a responsible autonomous being, you must consider yourself to be a moral being—an agent who can make moral claims against others. After all, what must a person be like to be capable of being a moral agent? He or she must be a rational person capable of making his or her own choices and willing to live by the consequences of the choices. In other words, a moral being is a rational autonomous agent—just the kind of being who is capable of entering into contracts. When you enter into a contract with another person, you are treating that person as a responsible autonomous contract maker. From the perspective of morality, parties to a contract are equals. Hence, arguing from a Kantian perspective, you must treat other contract makers in a similar way. You must recognize them as moral agents as well. As A. I. Melden would say, the act of promise making would establish a moral relation between moral agents.[5]

Premise 3 is the key to the argument. It asserts that one can be a moral agent only if he or she has rights that can be pressed as claims against others. The essential concepts in a defense of this premise are responsibility, dignity, and rights. A responsible being is a being who can make choices according to his or her own insights. He or she is not under the control of others. He or she does not live simply for another. In other words, a responsible person is a person who has dignity and self-respect. But one has dignity and self-respect when one can assert oneself in the world. One can only have dignity and self-respect if one can say such things as "I may be wrong, but I am entitled to my opinion," "I will not change the research results because such behavior would violate the code

---

[5] See A. I. Melden, *Rights and Persons* (Berkeley and Los Angeles: University of California Press, 1977), esp. Chapter 2.

of professional ethics which I have voluntarily adopted," "What I do on my free time is none of the company's business." In uttering these remarks, one is asserting rights claims since rights are moral entitlements. What I have been arguing is that a person must be a rights bearer if he or she is to be a moral agent in the complete sense. The following quotation captures my point exactly:

> Rights, we are suggesting, are fundamental moral commodities because they enable us to stand up on our own two feet, "to look others in the eye," and to feel in some fundamental way the equal of anyone. To think of oneself as the holder of rights is not to be unduly but properly proud, to have that minimal self-respect that is necessary to be worthy of the love and esteem of others. Conversely, to lack the concept of oneself as a rights bearer is to be bereft of a significant element of human dignity. Without such a concept, we could not view ourselves as beings entitled to be treated as not simply means but ends as well.[6]

Let me review the argument thus far. One can enter a valid business contract only if one is a responsible autonomous adult. But a responsible autonomous adult is the paradigm case of a moral agent. One can be a moral agent, however, only if one has rights that can be pressed against others. Therefore a person who enters a valid business contract is a person who has rights.

The remainder of the argument is rather simple. Premise 5 represents nothing more than the straightforward application of the moral principle of universalizability. What counts as a reason in one case must count as a reason in relevantly similar cases. The argument for our conclusion that persons entering a business contract must recognize the rights claims of others is now established as both valid and sound. Since the relation between an employer and an employee is essentially a contractual one, the thesis that an employer must recognize that his or her employees have certain rights has been established. Our analysis has shown that a focal point for any discussion of worker dignity in the corporation must be employee rights.

If the argument of this chapter is successful, something fairly significant has been achieved. The view of those who argue that ethics is not central to business practice has been refuted. Indeed, using the Kantian perspective (a central tradition in ethics), I have maintained that ethics is essential to business practice. Moreover, the ethical concerns that are central are just the ones that are fundamental to the neoclassical definition of the function of the corporation, namely, the demands of justice (fair play) and respect for individual rights.

---

[6] Norman E. Bowie and Robert L. Simon, *The Individual and the Political Order* (Englewood Cliffs, N.J.: Prentice-Hall, Inc., 1977), p. 78.

Several complications remain to be discussed. First, something must be done to make the phrase "respect for individual rights" more determinate. As it stands, it does not provide much guidance to managers and business executives concerned with the moral constraints on business practice. Second, various criticisms of the Kantian perspective must be addressed.

To establish the conclusion that contractees must recognize the rights of other contractees is one thing. To decide what such recognition would amount to is something else. In this section, I shall propose one analysis of what would constitute appropriate recognition. Our focus on contracts will continue to serve us well. Contract makers must look upon each other as rights bearers. What human right is closely associated with contract making? Surely it is the right to liberty. One cannot conclude a valid contract unless one is free to do so. That the market economy presupposes at least a negative right to liberty is accepted by almost the entire spectrum of political opinion from libertarians to welfare democrats.

To move from the claim that every human has a right to liberty to a list of specifications as to what the right to liberty entails is a difficult enterprise. In the most general formulation, the right to liberty is a right to noninterference. But obviously that right to noninterference is not open ended. We are not free to do whatever we want. The classic specification of a right to liberty is provided by John Stuart Mill:

> The sole end for which mankind are warranted individually or collectively in interfering with the liberty of action of any of their number is self-protection. That the only purpose for which power can be rightfully exercised over any member of a civilized community, against his will, is to prevent harm to others. His own good, either physical or mental, is not a sufficient warrant.[7]

The concept of harm provides a wide escape clause, however. Corporations could and indeed have argued that apparent violations of individual liberty are necessary to prevent harm to the corporation. On the basis of that argument, companies have regulated the dress, social life, family life, and political opinions of employees. Any employee action that adversely affects profit "harms" the corporation and could be restricted. The problems are not just theoretical. Let me amplify this analysis with some practical questions raised by the senior vice president of a major life insurance company as we discussed the issue of employee rights. Suppose that an employee of a major private health insurance company exercises his or her free speech to lobby actively for the passage of a government

---

[7] John Stuart Mill, *On Liberty*, ed. Currin V. Skield (Indianapolis, Ind.: Bobbs-Merrill Library of Liberal Arts, 1956), p. 13.

health insurance bill that would eliminate private health insurance companies. In effect, this employee seeks the elimination of his or her job and the jobs of colleagues. Does the insurance company or his or her employer have a right to constrain the employee's freedom of speech in this case? Consider freedom of religious conscience. Suppose that a life insurance company acquires a health insurance company. This health insurance company pays medical bills for abortions. The claims processor from the parent company is a member of a church that holds abortion to be a deadly sin. On grounds of religious conscience, the processor refuses to process claims for medical expenses to cover abortion. Does the company have a right to fire this person, and if the company did, would it violate the employee's freedom of religious conscience?

What these examples show is that apparently one must balance the harm caused when a corporation denies an employee an opportunity to exercise one of his or her liberties against the harm done to profits if the corporation does not deny the employee that opportunity. Such balancing must often be done if the employee's exercise of his or her liberty would not violate Mill's condition. Does this mean that companies have unlimited justification for limiting employee freedom of action whenever profits are adversely affected? I think not.

Business activity takes place within a social framework. Society permits business to seek profits only insofar as business plays by the rules that society establishes. Hence, business activity should conform to the laws and basic moral norms of society. Once this background condition is understood, a business cannot restrict the freedom of an employee when that restriction requires the employee to perform some act that violates either the law or a basic moral norm of society. An employee cannot be ordered to falsify experimental data relating to product safety or to discriminate against a fellow employee on the basis of race. The fact that the falsification of the data or the discrimination would improve profits is irrelevant.

But what about restrictions on individual liberty that do not violate fundamental moral norms or statutes of law? Some further specification of the extent of a person's right to liberty is provided by the Constitution. As you recall, David Ewing was quoted in Chapter 1 as indicating that the constitutional rights of employees were not sufficiently protected in the marketplace. Such a gap in the protection of the Constitution for individual citizens seems unjustified. Since business activity takes place within American society, presumably business activity should be conducted consistent with the Bill of Rights, which specifies our right to liberty. For example, the rights to free speech and to freedom of religious conviction are specific examples of the rights to liberty that are embodied in the Constitution. As such, these rights should be honored by business practice.

The recognition of these constitutional rights by business would result in major changes in business pratice at least in many firms. The insurance company employee's right to lobby for an insurance bill that would eliminate private companies is more fundamental than the insurance company's desire not to have the issue discussed. Indeed, in this case I would argue that the insurance company has no rights claims which are relevant in this case. The employee is not interfering with the company's right to do business and the company has a right of free speech equal to that of the employee to bring its case before the American public. It is interesting to note that the legal issue surrounding this case has already been settled. Section 387 of the *Restatement of Agency* defines the employee's duty of loyalty. The law denies that the employee's duty necessarily extends outside his employment. To illustrate this point the law uses the very case we have been discussing:

> A, employed by P, a life insurance company, in good faith advocates legislation which would require a change in the policies issued by the company. A has violated no duty to P.[8]

On similar grounds I would argue that an employee's duty to loyalty does not require that he or she buy a Chrysler automobile just because he or she is working for Chrysler. Except in very rare circumstances, for example in intelligence work or in the locksmith trade, an employee cannot be forbidden to visit certain bars or other legal places of amusement, pool halls or massage parlors. Outside the workplace, the employee's constitutionally guaranteed rights should far more often override any right of an employer to prevent employee conduct which might reflect adversely on the employer's business.

Even within the work place, constitutionally protected rights should be given a more prominent place. Surely the employee who objects to processing abortion claims can be accommodated. Someone else can do the abortion claims, while he or she takes on the claim processing responsibilities that someone else is now doing. Indeed greater flexibility in scheduling and job description could protect employee rights, reduce role conflicts for working mothers, and perhaps even increase morale, productivity, and profit.

But what about those difficult cases in which the rights of employees clash with the rights of management? After all, the employer is a party to the contract between employer and employee, and the contract argument works just as well in establishing employer rights as it does in establishing

---

[8] Quoted from Phillip I. Blumberg, "Corporate Responsibility and the Employee's Duty of Loyalty and Obedience," in *Ethical Theory and Business,* eds. Thomas Beauchamp and Norman E. Bowie (Englewood Cliffs, N.J.: Prentice-Hall, Inc., 1979), p. 307.

employee rights. For example, in Chapter 1, it was argued that within certain constraints corporations have a moral right to loyalty. It is also an established point at law that an employer has a legal right to loyalty. This right is captured in the so-called law of agency. For example, Section 387 of the Restatement of Agency expresses the general principle that

> *an agent is subject to a duty to his principle to act solely for the benefit of the principle in all matters connected with his agency.*[9]

Specifically, "the agent is also under a duty not to act or speak disloyally"[10] and the agent is to keep confidential any information acquired by him as an employee that might damage the agent or his business.

In other words, society does give a business a right to pursue profit as well as give individuals a right to free action. The interesting and difficult practical situations occur when rights come into conflict. For example, what about dress codes that an employer believes the image of his business requires?

In any case recognition of the intractability of certain ethical issues does not imply that no discussions on such issues should be made or, even that after listening to the counsels of despair, that one decision is as good as any other. What can be done?

The Notion of Procedural Justice

Philosophical analysis need not leave these questions completely unanswered. The work of John Rawls enables us to raise additional considerations toward resolving such questions. Consider the following situations. Three brothers have been given a cake. How should the cake be distributed? If one supposes that there is no special difference among the brothers (e.g., that one has diabetes), should not the distribution be equal? What procedure would bring the equal distribution about? Would it not be plausible to argue that the procedure of making the person who cuts the cake receive the last piece is the best procedure for securing the morally desirable result? In this case, we have an example of what Rawls calls perfect procedural justice. Both the procedure and the end results are just.

Suppose that you are the state official responsible for setting up a state lottery. How would you exercise your responsiblity? Would not your

---

[9] Ibid., p. 308.
[10] Ibid., p. 307.

responsibility be fulfilled if you set up the lottery according to the accepted rules of fairness for games of chance? You would incur no moral blame whatsoever if the winner of the first lottery were the richest person in the state. The most that the state official can do is guarantee the fairness of the lottery procedures. Whoever wins the lottery has won fairly as long as the procedures were fair. Whenever fair procedures establish or define fair outcomes, one has an example of what Rawls calls pure procedural justice.

A final situation is provided when one considers criminal punishment. The ideal in terms of justice is to apprehend and punish all, but only, those persons who break the law. Unlike the cake example, there are practical impossibilities for creating a procedure that would bring about completely just results. One then seeks a procedure that approximates just results, for example, in retributive justice a procedure that specifically convicts guilty persons and protects innocent persons. In our own legal system, trial by jury constrained by procedural safeguards spelled out in our Constitution is the accepted procedure. Since that procedure does not yield perfect results, Rawls refers to it as imperfect procedural justice.

Of particular relevance to business ethics are the notions of pure and imperfect procedural justice. For many issues within business, there may be no agreement as to what results are right. For example, there may be no agreement as to whether John, James, or Jack deserves a certain promotion. A promotion procedure would be established, which in this case would be an instance of pure procedural justice. So long as the procedure is followed, the promotion is just. One might also use this procedural method to determine how to harmonize the interests of the corporation's various constituencies.

In other cases, one might know the result one wants but not know how to achieve it. Such cases would be analogous to the criminal justice example where procedures of imperfect justice might be used. One might desire that every product one manufactures be guaranteed free of defects; however, since that is a practical impossibility, one must adopt certain statistical procedures for quality control.

As we continue our exploration into business ethics, we will see that procedural solutions to ethical problems will be central. Of particular interest will be the discussion of self-regulation in Chapter 5. One problem of business ethics is to design a set of mutually acceptable procedures—a revised social contract—that would enable decisions on perplexing questions to be made.

Consider the conflicts among rights. First, it should be noted that the law of agency is in conformity with the contention of Chapter 1 that no employee can be required to perform some act that violates either law or a basic moral norm of society. The law of agency specifically states that "In no event would it be implied that an agent has a duty to perform acts which . . . are illegal or unethical."[11]

However, both the interpretation of rights claims and the adjudication among competing rights claims rest with the courts or with other appropriate procedural mechanisms, for example, the collective bargaining process. Moral philosophers cannot provide correct solutions to conflicting rights claims—neither can anyone else for that matter. As employees begin to press these rights claims, management has only two viable responses. It can allow the courts to resolve such matters, or it can provide the mechanism for resolving the conflicts within the corporate decision-making process itself.

The Ethics of Bluffing and Poker

Having made some effort to make the phrase "legitimate individual rights" more determinate, we turn now to some of the criticisms that have been leveled against the Kantian analysis of justice and the breaking of contracts. As you will recall, Kant argued that, if the maxim behind a proposed action cannot be universalized, then the action ought not be done. An action cannot be universalized if its general practice would be self-defeating (e.g., lying or cheating on exams).

But many would argue that certain types of lying can be universalized without being self-defeating and without being wrong. For example, the rules of poker permit the type of lying called bluffing. Moreover, such bluffing is not self-defeating, even though the rule permitting bluffing is universally accepted as part of the game. Successful games of poker take place all the time. Moreover, business practice is analogous to poker, and hence a considerable amount of deception is not only common but could be universalized without undermining business practice.

One of the classic expressions of this point of view is Albert Z. Carr's "Is Business Bluffing Ethical?" In that article, Carr maintains that the proper analogy for understanding business ethics is that of poker:

> *Poker's own brand of ethics is different from the ethical ideals of civilized human relationships. The game calls for distrust of the other fellow. It ignores the claim of friendship. Cunning deception and concealment of one's strength and intentions, not kindness and openheartedness, are vital in poker.*[12]

---

[11] Ibid.

[12] Albert Z. Carr, "Is Business Bluffing Ethical?" *Harvard Business Review,* (January–February 1968), 45.

As it is with poker, so it is with business:

> *Most executives from time to time are almost compelled in the interests of their companies or themselves to practice some form of deception when negotiating with customers, dealers, labor unions, government officials, or even the departments of their companies. By conscious misstatements, concealment of pertinent facts, or exaggeration—in short, by bluffing—they seek to persuade others to agree with them. . . . A good part of the time the businessman is trying to do unto others as he hopes others will not do unto him. . . . A man who intends to be a winner in the business game must have a game player's attitude.*[13]

Carr raises several important challenges to anyone discussing business ethics. Among the challenges that he raises are the following: (1) that the most appropriate analogy for understanding business is the game of poker, (2) that competition and negotiation require a form of deception that includes conscious misstatements and the concealment of pertinent facts, and (3) that a successful businessperson must "do unto others as he hopes others will not do unto him."These challenges will be discussed continually throughout the book.

Before responding to Carr's challenges, it seems important to indicate that Carr is not saying that business can ignore all moral rules. If it did, I think that Carr would agree with Kant that such a position would be self-defeating. However, Carr does think that business practice can and does require a great deal of deception: "conscious misstatements, concealment of pertinent facts, and exaggeration."

Moreover, one does not need extensive experience in business to know that there are many types of deception, like bluffing, that are both widely practiced and widely accepted. A few examples suffice. It is common knowledge that auto dealers do not expect people to pay the sticker price for automobiles. A certain amount of bargaining is taken for granted. The same is true for real estate prices. The asking price for a house is seldom the selling price. At the initial bargaining session, labor leaders also overstate wage demands, and management also understates the wage increases it is willing to grant. In all these instances, the final price or wage contract is arrived at through a process that does resemble the poker game Carr uses as an analogy. The price or wage contract does depend in part on the strength of one's hand and on one's bluffing ability. In the late 1970's, one did need to pay the sticker price for small foreign cars with good gas mileage.

Surely the auto dealers and sellers of homes cannot be accused of immoral behavior when they post prices above those that they are willing

---

[13] Ibid., p. 144.

to accept. Surely the labor leader is not behaving immorally when he overstates the wage increases that his union expects to receive.

But equally surely there are limits. Let us return to the real estate example. Suppose that I am willing to sell my home for $60,000 if that is the best price I can get. I ask $70,000. A potential buyer's initial offer is $60,000. I turn it down and tell him that $65,000 is my rock bottom price. He purchases the home for $65,000.[14]

Many people would characterize my behavior as shrewd bluffing rather than as an immoral lie. Most people would think more of me rather than less. However, suppose that I had manufactured the claim that someone else had promised me that they were in the process of writing up a contract for $65,000 for the house but that I would sell it to him since we were both members of Rotary International. In this case most people would agree that I had told an immoral lie. By the way, it would not improve the moral character of my action to have my brother pretend to make me an offer so that the prospective buyer would be pressured to actually buy. That would be a case of an immoral lie as well.

Sometimes how the vast majority of people feels about whether an action is a lie or merely bluffing cannot be determined. Consider the following examples from collective bargaining negotiations:

1. Management negotiators saying, "We can't afford this agreement," when it would not put the firm out of business but only reduce profits from somewhat above to somewhat below the industry average.
2. Union negotiators saying, "The union membership is adamant on this issue," when they know that, while one half of the membership is adamant, the other half couldn't care less.
3. Union negotiators saying, "If you include this provision, we'll get membership approval of the contract," when they know, that they'll have an uphill battle for approval even with the provision.[15]

Perhaps the debate on the line between harmless exaggeration and immoral deception is most intense in the discussion of advertising ethics. Horror stories concerning deceptive advertising abound. Language changes its meaning in many ads. "Noncancellable" and "guaranteed renewable" have technical meanings not at all what one would expect. Often age stipulations are thrown in. The physical world is subject to optical illusions that the advertiser can exploit as well. Marketing research has shown that, if housewives are given the choice between two boxes of

---

[14] These examples are adopted from Thomas L. Carson and Richard E. Wokutch, "Ethical Perspectives on Lying, Deception and Bluffing in Business," unpublished manuscript, pp. 1–2. (see below)

[15] Ibid., pp. 3–4.

This paper was delivered at a conference on Business and Professional Ethics at Kalamazoo College and Western Michigan University in November 1979.

cereal, one short and squat and the other tall and narrow, they will almost invariably choose the tall and narrow box, even if it contains less and costs more. Boxes and bottles are often much larger than needed for the quantity of material contained therein. Testimonials, until recently, were also under attack. And so it goes. To many, these practices indicate that advertising is an inherently deceptive industry.

Yet others would argue that much of what critics call "deceptive advertising" is nothing more than harmless bluffing. They argue that the purpose of advertising is to sell a product. To sell a product, you must put a product in its best light, you must emphasize its good points, you must exaggerate a bit. So long as this commercial context is understood, exaggeration, puffery, and hyperbole are not deceptive. The claim that one's product is the best or the use of other such superlatives should not cause anyone problems. Jules Henry speaks of the philosophy guiding the commercial context as the pecuniary philosophy. In the pecuniary philosophy, there is something known as pecuniary truth. A pecuniary pseudotruth is a false statement made as if it were true, but not intended to be believed. "No proof is offered for a pecuniary truth and no one looks for it." As Henry puts it,

> No sane American would think that literally everybody is "talking about the new Starfire," that Alpine cigarettes literally "put the men in menthol smoking," or that a woman wearing a Distinction foundation garment becomes so beautiful that her sisters literally want to kill her.[16]

Of course, some could criticize the whole commercial context and the so-called pecuniary philosophy that accompanies it. However, the critics should note that something like the pecuniary philosophy seems deeply embedded within human nature. Almost all of us try to sell ourselves. Whether searching for a job or searching for a mate, we engage in exaggeration, puffery, and hyperbole about ourselves. And we expect others to do the same. We also use the pecuniary language to talk about our children, our jobs, our neighborhoods, or our spouses. (Note that, for the last three items, hyperbole can be negative as well as positive.) Perhaps the world would be a better place if human beings could avoid hyperbole or puffery. Since such a change in human nature is unlikely, perhaps it would be more realistic to accept the pecuniary philosophy as operative in the commercial context—as well as elsewhere—and to discuss various rules or principles that might constrain pecuniary philosophy.

With these thoughts in mind, we need some criteria to distinguish the relatively harmless cases of puffery from the immoral lies and deceptions. A lie might be defined as a false statement uttered with the intention to

---

[16] Jules Henry, "Advertising as a Philosophical System," in Thomas Beauchamp and Norman E. Bowie, p. 470.

mislead. The addition of the intentionality condition is extremely important. It allows many false statements not to be lies. Fortunately, mistaken utterances, although false, are not lies; otherwise, most of us would be frequent, if not habitual, liars. It also exempts poets. "He has the heart of a lion" is not a lie, although it is surely false. Sometimes advertisements are akin to poetry. "Esso puts a tiger in your tank" is false, but surely it is not a lie.

The intentionality condition is useful in areas beyond poetry. The Supreme Court decided in favor of a Federal Trade Commission (FTC) ruling that determined that Colgate-Palmolive's ad that Rapid Shave could soften even the toughness of sandpaper was deceptive. The television commercial depicted someone shaving sandpaper that had been generously lathered with Rapid Shave. Now the FTC admitted that Rapid Shave could soften sandpaper so that it could be shaved. However, the sandpaper needed to soak in Rapid Shave for approximately eighty minutes before it could be shaved. On the basis of this, the FTC declared the ad deceptive because the television viewer was deceived into believing that the actual experiment was being shown; the viewer was not informed about the eighty-minute wait.

Colgate-Palmolive disagreed that there was any deception. It compared its "experiment" with the use of mashed potatoes instead of ice cream in all television ice cream ads. Just as the television lights made the use of ice cream impossible, so the working time made an actual experiment impossible. The court turned down the analogy on the grounds that the mashed potatoes prop was not being used for additional proof of the quality of the product while the Rapid Shave commercial certainly was trying to provide additional proof. Perhaps the Rapid Shave decision could be generalized to make the following point: Within that pecuniary context, any deception or false statement that is not related to the cost, amount, or quality of the product is not an example of immoral deception in advertising. Such a principle would enable us to focus on the context in which advertising takes place.

Yet another criterion could be stated as follows: Any exaggeration that would not deceive the rational person is not inappropriate. No rational person will believe that the foam on Old Froshingslosh beer will really be on the bottom. (Whether such deception would be immoral within some other context is not a matter for discussion here.) Deception in advertising involves the use of false statements or inaccurate depictions of a product that are material to the consumer's decision to purchase and that are undertaken intentionally to mislead rational consumers. On that account, most advertising is not deceptive. However, equally on that account some advertising is deceptive and, more important, some advertising or marketing practices are deceptive. Packaging techniques are surely one example of a practice that deceives in terms of amount.

But what counts as a rational consumer? The federal agency that has confronted this question head on is the Federal Trade Commission. The commission has drawn a distinction between the rational consumer and the ignorant consumer. The ignorant consumer takes everything literally. He or she really does believe that, when Old Froshingslosh beer advertises that the foam will be on the bottom, it really will be on the bottom. The ignorant consumer does not show any common sense. It is generally agreed that, to require business practice to be so open and literal that even the ignorant consumer would not be deceived would stifle business and seriously affect productivity. On that point, the conventional wisdom seems correct. However, the definition of the "rational consumer" is fairly amorphous. Sometimes "rational consumer" is just a synonym for "average consumer." Advertisements, like television programs, would have to be aimed at those with the reading ability of a twelve-year-old. At other times "rational consumer" is given a more normative definition. It is equated with what a consumer should know. Perhaps the normative definition puts more responsibility on the consumer than does the definition that appeals to the average consumer.

Another way to handle this debate over where to draw the line between misstatement and fraud is to appeal to a criterion of public openness. A business practice is not deceptive when that business acknowledges the rules it is playing under. The ads for the auto dealers and for real estate make it perfectly clear that the "asking price" is not the "real price." An ad for a home that says "Asking $120,000" virtually announces that the homeowner is in a mood to deal. Auto ads for individual dealers stress the fact that they will match any other deal in town. They explicitly acknowledge the bargaining aspect of auto sales. Grocery store ads by and large contain none of this bargaining language. The price of oranges is not a function of an individual bargain worked out between the individual purchaser and the supermarket.

Deception enters when a businessperson announces that he or she is playing by one set of rules when in fact he or she is playing by another. Of course immorality also enters when one partner to a contract breaks his or her end. But, so long as the rules of the game are known, then most people will accept consequences of business practice that they might not accept in other circumstances. Consider the following case:

The Leaking Valve[17]

The Hawley Corporation, which ranks among the nation's one hundred largest manufacturing firms, had a persistent problem with a leaking valve assembly on the hydraulic presses it makes and distributes. Unable to remedy the

---

[17] This case and the subsequent case, "A Big Break for Fenwick Creations," was prepared by the Committee for Education in Business Ethics under a grant from the National Endowment for the Humanities.

defect on its own, Hawley engineers called in several vendors of this type of assembly and described the problem to them. The Hawley group explained that it hoped that the vendors would be willing to find a solution to the problem but that corporate policy did not permit paying for this sort of developmental work done outside the company.

Only one of the vendor firms, Allbright, Inc., decided to proceed on this basis with developing something that could answer Hawley's difficulty. Allbright reasoned that if it produced the remedy it would be in an excellent position to get the contract for supplying Hawley with the improved assembly.

The engineering department of the two firms worked together, and after a fairly lengthy effort a modification of the Hawley assembly was perfected that eliminated the leaking.

The Hawley purchasing department then sent out requests for bids on the new assembly to a number of vendors, Allbright included. Reston Corporation underbid Allbright and was awarded the order by Hawley.

Most of my students who analyze this case agree that Allbright had no right to the contract. Their argument is almost always the same: The rules were known and hence Allbright knew it was taking a risk when it agreed to assist Hawley.

One should compare this case with another.

_____ A Big Break for Fenwick Creations _____

Fenwick Creations, a manufacturer of men's and women's sportswear, had come up with an exceptionally well-designed new line of clothes for tennis, jogging, and cycling. Initial response from buyers was so favorable that Fenwick's sales managers thought they had a good chance of finally attaining one of their goals: to get their merchandise into the locally prestigious Wilton-Cool and Company department store.

Wilton-Cool was known in the trade for acceptance of new lines. It was also known for making acceptance contingent upon special incentives from suppliers.

Fenwick's sales office offered to guarantee the resale of Wilton-Cool's total order, within a period of time agreeable to the department store. Fenwick offered further to take Wilton-Cool's statement about sales without a check of inventories by Fenwick.

Wilton-Cool accepted the proposition and ordered 500 articles of sportswear from Fenwick. After the previously arranged termination date, the department store claimed to have sold 325 of the items. In fact, 450 had been sold; but Fenwick abided by the guarantee. It was understood on both sides—though never stated—that what had occurred was standard practice and that prices charged by the supplier took these costs into account.

In this case, most of my students do not accept the morality of the practice. Even though the two businesses, Fenwick and Wilton-Cool, were aware of the rules, other relevant parties were not. The consumers were particularly adversely affected. Consumers believe that, in a competitive market economy, purchase decisions among businesses are made on the basis of quality and price. Those are the operative rules of the game. But clearly these rules are being violated in this case.

We now have a much better handle on what we mean by deceptive advertising. Deceptive advertising is advertising that is intentionally designed to mislead the rational consumer who knows the rules of the game about the cost, amount, or quality of a product.

But how does this discussion of advertising fit in with our larger analysis of the Kantian argument against lying. It does show that not all cases of "lying" will run afoul of the categorical imperative. Some types of "lies" can be universalized without being self-defeating. There are a few passages in Kant's writings where Kant himself seems to recognize the limitations of his views.

> *Again, I may make a false statement (falsiloquium) when my purpose is to hide from another what is in my mind and when the latter can assume that such is my purpose, his own purpose being to make a wrong use of the truth. Thus, for instance, if my enemy takes me by the throat and asks where I keep my money, I need not tell him the truth, because he will abuse it; and my untruth is not a lie (mendacium) because the thief knows full well that I will not, if I can help it, tell him the truth and that he has no right to demand it of me.*[18]

Nonetheless, there are clear instances of deceptive and fraudulent practices that do undermine the enterprise of business itself. The breaking of contracts and theft are paradigm cases. Such activities do run afoul of Kant's categorical imperative. It is clear that Kant would allow far less in the way of deceptive bluffing than would Carr. In Kantian language, Kant has a much higher number of business practices that he thinks would be self-defeating if universalized than does Carr. Let us now consider the dispute between Carr and Kant empirically. What business practices, if they became more common, would undermine business practice itself?

Let us take Carr's analogy seriously. Should the stockholders applaud a chief executive officer whose operating procedure is analogous to the operating procedure of a poker player? In Carr's view, "A good part of the time the businessman is trying to do unto others as he hopes others will not do unto him." But surely such a practice is very risky. The danger of discovery is great, and our experience of the past several years indicates that many corporations that have played the game of business like the game of poker have suffered badly. Moreover, if business practice

---

[18] Immanuel Kant, *Lectures on Ethics,* trans. Louis Infield (New York: Harper & Row, Publishers, 1963), p. 227.

consisted essentially of these conscious misstatements, exaggerations, and the concealment of pertinent facts, it seems clear that business practice would be inherently unstable. Contemporary business practice presupposes such stability, and business can only be stable if the chief executive officer has a set of moral standards higher than those that govern the game of poker.

This philosophical point, that deception must be very limited if society is to be stable, has been enriched by the appearance of Dr. Sissela Bok's book, *Lying: Moral Choice in Public and Private Life,* which reaffirms the centrality of the moral rule, "Do not lie." One of the points Dr. Bok most emphatically makes is that the existence of society itself depends upon the acceptance by the members of society of the rule "Do not lie."

> *trust in some degree of veracity functions as a foundation of relations among human beings; when this trust shatters or wears away, institutions collapse. ... A society, then, whose members were unable to distinguish truthful messages from deceptive ones, would collapse. But even before such a general collapse, individual choice and survival would be imperiled. The search for food and shelter could depend on no expectations from others. A warning that a well was poisoned or a plea for help in an accident would come to be ignored unless independent confirmation could be found.*[19]

Dr. Bok's point can be restated so that it applies specifically to business.

Central to the philosophy of most businesspersons is the view that government should not intrude extensively into business. With respect to business, *laissez-faire* is the dominant view. However, even those with libertarian philosophies allow one important function to government. Government is to be the police officer that enforces the rules of business activity. Most important, government is to uphold the sanctity of contracts. This view is expressed clearly in the classical treatment of the merits of capitalism.

However, if business activity is to thrive, most people most of the time must uphold voluntarily the sanctity of contracts. No government can serve as an omnipresent police officer. Indeed, even within the competitive marketplace, the basic moral nature of persons must be assumed. Usually, people will keep to their contracts even when it does not work out to their advantage to do so. If this were not true, law enforcement would soon become impossibly burdensome. Indeed, we assume that even with limited cheating at least the police are honest. The uncovering of a dishonest cop is always a great shock. Commerce requires a basically honest society and honest police.

---

[19] Sissela Bok, *Lying: Moral Choice in Public and Private Life* (New York: Pantheon Books, 1978), pp. 19, 31.

A cause of growing concern is the increased cheating on the part of an increasing number of citizens. Internal revenue spokespersons fear that, as American citizens face higher taxes through inflation and as they hear of cheating by others, they will tend to cheat on their own taxes. Internal revenue officials concede that enforcement agents could not deal with widespread cheating and that such a situation would undermine the income tax system. One need not wait for the collapse of the income tax to observe breakdowns in the market that result from breakdowns in the obligation to the sanctity of contracts.

Shoplifting has approached epidemic proportions. Since shoplifters are difficult to apprehend and even more difficult to convict, a partial "solution" is to figure into the retail price of a good a certain markup to cover the cost of shoplifting. The result is an increase on the price of goods. Of course as prices rise, one would expect shoplifting to increase. This is especially true when people realize that a portion of the price of their goods is set aside to cover shoplifting. Why shouldn't they shoplift, too, if they are already paying the cost of the shoplifters who shoplift with impunity?

If such a view becomes widespread, the market system will break down just the way a rationing scheme does when cheating is both widely known about and goes unpunished. Suppose that there is a ban on watering the lawn that is not enforced. Sam, who has followed the ban but who sees all his neighbors water the lawn, will be silly if he continues to refrain from watering his lawn. As a result, the rationing system breaks down.

All of this is fairly obvious. Bok's most significant point is that rather minor acts of deception like white lies, puffery, and exaggeration all contribute to a general instability. In other words, Carr underestimates the undesirable effects of such practices. If I were to summarize Bok's book in one sentence, I would say, "Even white lies, flattery, and deceptive practices that are *publicly known and accepted* undermine social institutions." Bok's critique of "white lies" and the use of placebos applies equally well to deception in business:

> *Triviality surely does set limits to when moral inquiry is reasonable. But when we look more closely at practices such as placebo-giving, it becomes clear that all lies defended as "white" cannot be so easily dismissed. In the first place, the harmlessness of lies is notoriously disputable. What the liar perceives as harmless or even beneficial may not be so in the eyes of the deceived. Second, the failure to look at an entire practice rather than at their own isolated case often blinds liars to cumulative harm and expanding deceptive activities. Those who begin with white lies can come to resort to more frequent and more serious ones. Where some tell a few white lies, others may tell more. Because lines are so hard to draw, the indiscriminate use of such lies can lead to other deceptive practices. The aggregate harm from a large number of marginally harmful instances may, therefore, be*

highly undesirable in the end—for liars, those deceived, and honesty and trust more generally.[20]

In Bok's view even the bluffing that goes on in real estate and auto sales has its dangers. So does the hyperbole that accompanies advertising and the excessive demands that are characteristic of the early stages of collective bargaining negotiations. Those of us in academic life can see Bok's point when we consider what has happened as the result of grade inflation and the inflating of letters of recommendation. The professional and graduate schools are suspicious of high grades. Hardly anyone takes letters of recommendation seriously anymore.

In the area of business, a number of parents, like myself, have simply taught our children to regard all advertising as deceptive. Often, that type of teaching is not difficult. After eating three boxes of cereal so that one can send three box tops and 50 cents for a marvelous Star Wars toy, the toy almost never seems worth it. Children learn the lesson early. Jokes about used car salesmen are so ingrained in the public that honest used car ads just aren't taken seriously.

The growth of the large firm, the complexity of business decisions, the need for planning and stability, and the undesirable effects of puffery, exaggeration, and deception all count against Carr's view that the ethics of business should be the ethics of a poker game. Just how much puffery and exaggeration business practice can permit without serious undesirable consequences is a matter for further empirical investigation.

But how much deception, exaggeration, and puffery should business practice permit? We will have to leave a more comprehensive answer to that question until Chapter 4, where some business practices like competition are considered in more detail. One condition that seemed to distinguish legitimate from illegitimate bluffing in our earlier examples was whether or not all parties knew that bluffing was taking place. The bluffing that goes on in used-car lots is legitimate because everyone knows that asking prices are just that. This openness condition, as I chose to call it, is often the basis for legislation as well. People should be free to speculate in stocks, but if an accountant, lawyer, or other person obtains inside information, that person is not free to buy or sell the stock of that company or the stock of any other company that would be significantly affected if the inside information were publicly known. In a context in which bluffing and exaggeration are permitted, open access to all relevant information is a moral necessity. Otherwise, the rules of the bluffing game are unfair. Poker is unfair when some of the players do not know the rules that are being used.

---

[20] Ibid., p. 60.

Summary

In our examination of role morality in Chapter 1, the analysis indicated that a morality based on my station and its duties was not sufficient for settling issues in business ethics. Role morality was deficient because there is no perspective from within role morality for settling conflicts among roles. Moreover, our settled moral convictions indicate that role morality's obligations frequently ought to be overridden by the obligations of a more general morality. Both in Chapter 2 and in this chapter, I have attempted to buttress role morality with some considerations from traditional moral theory. In general, we have seen that the obligations and responsibilities associated with one's job (one's vocational role) must be consistent with (1) the purposes and functions of business practice, (2) the basic standards of justice required for all cooperative human activity, and (3) the legitimate individual rights claims and the basic dignity and self-respect of all persons. This overall account, which includes the universal moral norms for business practice, a neoclassical definition of the function of a corporation, and a theory of role morality, will go far in providing a theoretical framework for business ethics.

In Chapter 4, we will consider some of the commonly accepted rules of business practice to determine which do and which do not meet the standards for ethical business practice.

An Ethical Analysis of "Competition" and Consumer Sovereignty

It now can be taken as established that business practice presupposes a commitment on the part of businesspersons to adhere to minimum standards of justice and to acknowledge the appropriate rights of all those who participate in or are affected by business practice. However, these minimum moral rules hardly exhaust a description of the ethical issues that arise in standard business practice. The purpose of this chapter is to discuss some of these other issues. Of course, in a book of this length, it is impossible to discuss all the ethical issues that arise in standard business practice. I have selected two issues that are central to the growing literature on business ethics and are highly controversial. First, if competition is morally legitimate, what constraints govern its practice? Second, is consumer sovereignty the legitimate concept for determining what ought to be produced?

Competition and Its Role in Business

There is little doubt concerning the high regard given competition by business leaders. This quotation from Theodore Levitt can serve as an example:

> *If the all-out competitive prescription sounds austere or harsh, that is only because we persist in judging things in terms of utopian standards. Altruism,*

self-denial, charity, and similar values are vital in certain walks of our life—areas which, because of that fact, are more important to the long-run future than business. But for the most part those virtues are alien to competitive economics.

To the extent that there is conflict, can it not be a good thing? Every book, every piece of history, even every religion testifies to the fact that conflict is and always has been the subject, origin, and life blood of society. Struggle helps to keep us alive, to give élan to life. We should try to make the most of it, not avoid it.[1]

Despite such accolades, the chief virtue of competition in the business setting is instrumental. Competition draws out the best in people so that efficiency is achieved. Competition is a device for maximizing profit. Hence its value is instrumental rather than intrinsic. (A few people sound as if they regard competition as valuable in itself, but under scrutiny even those persons are most impressed with its instrumental value.)

In discussing competition, the economic definition must be distinguished from the psychological one. The economic definition is a technical one concerning the ability of one business firm to affect price.

"Perfect competition" exists only in the case where no farmer, businessman, or laborer is a big enough part of the total market to have any personal influence on market price.[2]

Competition of this type is rare as one might expect by having it called "pure competition." Moreover, modern corporations are not in favor of pure competition, despite the official rhetoric.

The other definition of competition that I call the psychological definition is much more central both to business practice and to business rhetoric. Two or more individuals compete with one another when they consciously strive to attain a scarce resource such as a promotion. In their conscious striving, they are well aware of the conscious striving of others; once one person has attained the scarce resource, he or she is considered the winner and the others are considered losers. To the extent that we can speak of groups of individuals such as teams and businesses as if they were individuals, we can speak of such entities as competing. Thus at the beginning of the baseball season all the teams compete to be the winner of the World Series. Companies compete to obtain contracts or to sell more of their products. Individuals compete to become the chief executive of a corporation.

---

[1] Theodore Levitt, "The Dangers of Social Responsibility," *Harvard Business Review*, 36 (September–October 1958), 49–50.

[2] Paul Samuelson, *Economics*, 9th ed. (New York: McGraw-Hill Book Company, 1973), p. 43.

Competition is a means for distributing scarce resources. Why should competition be selected as the appropriate means? Perhaps an analogy will illustrate the type of justification that most businesspersons would give for competition. Suppose that the world championship in baseball was decided not by a series between the two winners of the two leagues but rather by lottery, with all league participants having an equal chance. In such a system, there would still be baseball games and standings, but the world champion would not necessarily be one of the teams that won the most games. What could be said about baseball if it were organized in this way?[3]

First, there would be little reason for the teams to try to do their best. After all, baseball requires a lot of energy, and to perform proficiently a lot of practice is required as well. Moreover, some plays like crashing into walls, diving into dugouts, and sliding into home plate are physically dangerous. Why should a player risk making dangerous plays when the world championship is decided by lottery? Without the prize, there is no incentive to excel.

Second, baseball organized in such a way would not provide people with what they want. People want excellence exhibited in spectacular fielding, hard hitting, and reckless base running. Excellence in performance or function is highly valued. As we have seen, a lottery system is unlikely to provide the incentive to inspire excellence and hence to give people what they want.

Third, to settle the world championship on the basis of the lottery would violate the moral principle of "to each according to his merit." The teams that win the most games should compete for the championship. They have earned it. Competition provides a test for merit. Those who win the prizes through competition merit them.

These arguments, which seem so persuasive in the baseball example, are the same ones that sound persuasive to businesspersons when they speak of the competition for the "prizes" of economic goods and services. Competition spurs individuals to do their best. In part, doing one's best means doing things more efficiently, thereby increasing the stock of available goods and services. In another sense, doing one's best means excelling in terms of the quality of what one does. Competition provides the incentive for producing a high-quality product. The existence of alternative sources of supply serves as a kind of product control since these alternatives are a threat to companies that are tempted to shave quality for a greater profit. Finally, those who produce more and/or better deserve more of the scarce goods and services that the fruits of their labor can produce. Competition serves as a meritocratic device for allocating

---

[3] The idea that a competitive system can be usefully contrasted to a lottery was suggested to me by Robert L. Simon.

scarce resources. In summary, competition is justified on both utilitarian grounds and on grounds of justice. Competition enables efficient high-quality production and hence brings about the greatest good for the greatest number. By serving as a meritocratic device, it conforms to canons of justice by enabling those who deserve more to receive more.

Competition and Equal Opportunity However, business institutions, like other American institutions in which competition plays a major role, recognize that the competitive process must be subject to certain constraints if it is to prove morally acceptable. This point must be granted if a competitive situation is to be distinguished from a brawl. Even the New York Stock Exchange or the Chicago Commodity Exchange is rule governed. What distinguishes competition from simply fighting? Surely it is the existence of a set of rules or constraints that structures "the fighting."[4]

First, if competition is to be fair, then the competitors must have equal opportunity to compete. A race is hardly fair if one of the ten runners has a five-pound weight attached to each foot. Society should ensure that every person has a fair start. This view is captured by the principle of equal opportunity. The principle of equal opportunity is central to the American creed, and business practice should conform to it. According to the principle of equal opportunity, persons with the same ability and talents and who expend roughly the same effort should have roughly the same prospects of success. Race, religion, sex, and family background should not be relevant to one's success or failure in the competitive struggle.

In thinking about what the principle of opportunity requires, however, terrible problems result. These problems are now apparent as business struggles with affirmative action requirements. Let us consider a few of the more complex issues. Consider the footrace example again. Although it is obviously unfair to place a five-pound weight on someone, we do accept certain inequalities as fair. There are height advantages and weight advantages that are accepted in all sports. Short people are seriously disadvantaged in basketball. In the competitive struggle for a higher standard of living, society accepts inequalities in intelligence and talent, even though persons impoverished in these respects are far less likely to succeed. What justifiable criteria exist for determining which disadvantages in the competitive struggle should be accepted and which ones should not be?

As a starting point, the following principles seem to reflect the thinking of many.

---

[4] I discovered this point in a yet unpublished paper by Gerald MacCallum. A lengthy discussion may be found in Roger Caillois, *Man, Play and Games* (New York: Glencoe Free Press 1961).

1. Natural differences among persons should be accepted; differences imposed by society should not be accepted.

2. Disadvantages for which the individual is responsible should be accepted. Differences for which the individual is not responsible should not be accepted.

Under these principles, a footrace is not unfair if people differ in terms of weight or sobriety at the starting line. It is unfair if people impose penalties for one's color or religious preference. Thus, in hiring practices the fact that more intelligent people are more readily hired does not mean that hiring practices are unfair. To pay people in terms of the number of strawberries they pick is not unfair, even if some people are more adept at picking strawberries than are others. A hiring practice is unfair, however, if blacks are systematically excluded. A salary policy is unfair if women doing the same work as men receive less pay.

Although most people agree that the two principles given reflect current policy concerning equal opportunity, it does not take much philosophical analysis to show that the principles are totally inadequate as they stand. First, the two principles are contradictory. If in fact individuals should only be held responsible for differences for which they are responsible (principle 2), then natural differences among persons should not be accepted (which contradicts principle 1). Second, principle 1 breaks the link between competition and justice. If natural differences like intelligence for which individuals are not responsible are allowed to count, how can the competitive process serve as a meritocratic allocative device? On balance, the least intelligent receive very little of the scarce goods and resources, but since they are not responsible for their lack of intelligence, on what grounds do they *deserve* receiving so little? Third, are any of the differences that are important in competition, and hence affect the results of competition, differences for which a person can be held responsible? Children who grow up in slum houses from broken homes without adequate medical or educational resources cannot compete successfully. These children in turn produce more children who live in similar squalor. This depressing cycle continues virtually unbroken generation after generation. There is no way that most persons from such backgrounds will be able to compete fairly for the economic prizes (goods and resources). This argument receives its most general and persuasive statement in the writing of John Rawls.

Perhaps some will think that the person with greater natural endowments deserves those assets and the superior character that made their development possible. Because he is more worthy in this sense, he deserves the greater advantages that he could achieve with them. This view, however, is surely incorrect. It seems to be one of the fixed points of our considered judgments that no one deserves his place in the distribution of native endowments, any more than one deserves one's initial starting place in society. The assertion that a man deserves the superior character that enables him to make the effort to cultivate his abilities is equally problematic; for his character depends in large part upon fortunate family and social circumstances for which he can claim no credit. The notion of desert seems not to apply to these cases. Thus the more advantaged representative man cannot say that he deserves and therefore has a right to a scheme of cooperation in which he is permitted to acquire benefits in ways that do not contribute to the welfare of others.[5]

If Rawls is right, many of the differences among persons (e.g., character) that have been seen as justifying the results of competitive allocation on meritocratic grounds can no longer do so. We cannot say that the lesser amount of goods and services received by the lazy person is something that he or she deserves.

Rawls' analysis raises some very disturbing questions since most of our social institutions (including economic ones) presuppose that people are basically autonomous and hence are responsible for what they do. The "rational man" standard used by the FTC presupposes that most people can detect puffery and hyperbole for what it is. The law has traditionally assumed that persons are responsible for the contracts they make and are also responsible for taking due care with the products they buy. You cannot blame the manufacturer of a power lawnmower if it is used to trim a hedge and the user cuts off a hand as a result. However, recent laws requiring "cooling-off periods" before certain sales agreements become binding, the increased use of the concept of strict liability in negligence suits, and the advent of no-fault auto insurance settlements—all reflect movement away from the view that people can and should be held responsible for what they do. If Rawls' analysis and recent practice that reflects it is correct, one of the central arguments for competition will be defeated. Competition cannot be viewed as a just allocative device. Persons no longer deserve being winners or losers in the competitive struggle. How one fares is largely a matter of luck, not merit.

The debate on the extent of individual autonomy and responsibility is one of the central issues in contemporary philosophy. Whatever consensus develops, putting that consensus into practice throughout our social institutions will have important wide-ranging consequences. These consequences will affect business practice as well. As of now, however, there is no consensus in the philosophical community or in society at large. Hence, one of the chief arguments for competition, namely, that competition rewards merit and hence promotes justice, is cast into doubt. That

---

[5] John Rawls, *A Theory of Justice* (Cambridge, Mass.: Harvard University Press, 1971), pp. 103–104.

leaves the utilitarian argument as the chief basis of support. However, most people (including most utilitarians) cannot ignore the issue of distributive justice that arises in a society where competition holds such a central place. Our analysis of competition coincides with our analysis of the definition of the proper function of the corporation: If a competitive profit-motivated system of business can be justified on moral grounds, that justification will only be successful if the business community recognizes that it is the moral obligation of some other social institution to promote and put into effect programs that achieve distributive justice.

A more immediate problem faces the business community. Even on the traditional criteria of equal opportunity, some groups have been discriminated against. What is to be done about those who have been discriminated against in the past? On the basis of past discrimination, should women and blacks receive special treatment now? Affirmative action programs force business to face this difficult issue. Difficulties from affirmative action programs result because they are directed primarily at correcting harms caused a generation or more ago. Neither the perpetrators nor the victims of the harm are actually present.

It is a general principle of both the law and morality that some people should not be singled out for either benefits or burdens unless such benefits or burdens are merited. Job quotas and some other forms of reverse discrimination violate this fundamental principle.

Suppose that a corporation has deliberately discriminated against blacks from 1941–1960. Suppose that we could identify ten blacks per year who could have been hired but were not. At ten blacks per year for twenty years, we have two-hundred blacks who have been victims of discrimination. In 1960, one of the blacks sues and proves that the corporation has discriminated. Suppose that the court rules as follows:

1. The corporation must cease and desist in its discrimination. From 1961, qualified blacks will be hired.
2. The corporation must, in recompense for the two-hundred blacks denied jobs in 1941–1960, admit between 1961 and 1980 two-hundred blacks who would not qualify for jobs under nonbiased criteria

Let us assume that economic conditions require that those two-hundred blacks replace two-hundred whites who would have been hired. Although the first part of the decision surely seems correct, the second part of the decision is more problematic. The link that connects recompense to the injured party has been broken. The injury was suffered by the two-hundred blacks not hired between 1941 and 1960. The benefit is derived by two-hundred blacks who do not qualify for the job but nonetheless are hired between 1961 and 1980. The burdens are not carried by the two-hundred whites who were less qualified but nonetheless were admitted in 1941–1960. Rather, the burdens are carried by the two-hundred qualified whites denied jobs between 1961 and 1980. This seems wrong because equality before the law is being denied.

The wrong is analogous to the wrong created in the following example. Jones and Smith are neighbors on Oak Street. Smith brings a civil suit against Jones for alleged wrongs. The case drags on and on. Finally, the court decides in Smith's favor. But, alas, Smith and Jones have died. Doe now lives in Jones's house and Fawn lives in Smith's house. So the court decides that Mr. Doe should pay Mr. Fawn. Such a decision would be absurd, yet how does it differ from the case just cited?

It might be argued that there is no difference. In many cases of both proven and unproven discrimination, the victims are either dead or are not identifiable as individual victims. The original victims of slavery and Jim Crow are mostly dead, although the legacy of these crimes lives on in the fact that many blacks are disadvantaged and are denied equal opportunity. Indeed, this argument concerning the victims of discrimination can now be generalized to cover all victims of poverty whatever their race or sex. We now return to the issue raised by Rawls. Many of the victims of poverty are analogous to the footrace contestants with the five-pound weights strapped to them. Not to provide a handicap for such persons seems unfair. However, providing special consideration for such persons in hiring and job promotion undercuts the economic and, hence, utilitarian advantages enumerated previously on behalf of competition. These advantages are maximized only if the most qualified are hired. In our example, this is not the case.

This discussion shows that society is rethinking what the principle of equal opportunity encompasses. When can we say that society has provided each participant a fair start? The elimination of prejudice and the establishment of a system of public education, which had been sufficient for the achievement of equality of opportunity in the past, are now recognized not to be sufficient. But no new consensus has emerged. Neither has any consensus emerged as to whether the burden (costs) for providing an expanded sense of equality of opportunity should fall on corporations (through hiring quotas) or on society as a whole (negative income tax, the federal government as the employer of last resort). However, this discussion does show that competition is certainly not fair in the absence of the traditional notion of equality of opportunity and that fairness requires an expanded notion of what conditions must hold if equal opportunity is to be achieved. However, until some consensus reemerges on the criterion for what counts as equal opportunity, the rule of competition will not be completely acceptable to many Americans.

Competition and Cooperation There are problems with the efficiency argument as well. It is not competition by itself that promotes efficiency. The most that can be claimed is that competitive processes successfully integrated with other processes is most efficient. One of the most important of these other processes is cooperation. The philosophy of corporate executives reflects this fact. That is why loyalty and team spirit hold such high places in the corporate value system. The world of dog-eat-dog competition is Hobbes's world of the war of all against all. In such a world, life is nasty, brutish, and short. The world of unbridled competition is the ultimately chaotic world. Obviously, the practice of business is impossible in a world where Hobbesian competition prevails. Even if one concedes the value of competition in promoting efficiency and excellence, one must concede similar values to cooperation.

John Rawls is the contemporary philosopher who has taken cooperation most seriously. Rawls argues that the good society is a social union. The key to a social union is the perspective that members of society take toward society. The members of a social union have shared goals and have loyalty to and appreciation for their common institutions. How does this common attitude come about? In the just society, individuals develop psychologically in ways that lead persons to have such attitudes. This development does not take place in some abstract entity called society; rather, it takes place within various social institutions that can in turn be characterized as social unions. In Rawls's view a good society is a social union of social unions. All social unions are characterized by the same features. Cooperation and a common sense of purpose are central.

> In much the same way that players have the shared end to execute a good and fair play of the game, so the members of a well-ordered society have the common aim of cooperating together to realize their own and another's nature in ways allowed by the principles of justice.[6]

Good business institutions should be social unions. If such language seems too idealistic for the harsh realities of business life, one might consider some of the recent developments in personnel management. Often there has been a gulf between labor and management. Each considered the other as an irritating antagonist if not an outright enemy. Each saw itself in competition with the other for scarce company resources. In some situations, circumstances have required a change in that point of view. Perhaps the most notable example is the Chrysler Corporation. Both sides recognized that cooperation between labor and management was a necessary condition for survival. Labor made a number of financial sacrifices. The president of the United Auto Workers obtained a seat on Chrysler's

---

[6] Ibid., p. 527.

board of directors. Both labor and management are actively cooperating to achieve a high level of quality control, particularly on the new K cars. In Japan, employees and employers usually constitute something akin to a family. Even in very bad times employers resist laying off employees. Employees have an intense sense of loyalty to their employer. In many countries there is an increasingly strong movement to shared employee–employer control in the decision-making process. Just how far all this will go is a matter of speculation. Such developments, however, confirm the philosophical point that the maximum amount of goods and services is not obtained solely by competition. Some balance of competition and cooperation is necessary. Hence it is not correct to say that competition by itself is the most efficient form of business practice.

Competition and Good Losers The utilitarian advantages of competition cannot accrue if people reject the notion of losing. If marathon runners are competing for the crown, there can be only one winner. If the losers did not accept their loss, but instead tried to cheat in future meets or to "do in" the winner, marathon racing would be a very different activity.

In business, there are a number of reasons to think that the competitive process yields losers as well as winners is overlooked. Some corporations faced with too many losses subscribe too readily to the philosophy "Winning isn't everything; it is the only thing." Falsification of experimental data, corner cutting on safety, shoddy advertising, and general corporate insensitivity prevail when a company suffers several setbacks in the competitive struggle. Some corporate officials then tend to view the world as "dog eat dog" and to think that "anything goes."

Such a view overlooks the considerations advanced in Chapter 2. A corporation is charted by society to promote the common good. It is not charted to promote its own survival regardless of the cost to society. Just as in football and ice hockey, there are certain limits to the measures one can take to win the game. There is a recognized concept of playing dirty, and playing dirty is morally condemned. There is a concept of playing dirty in business as well. Businesspersons are not permitted to play dirty when faced with loss. Business executives gladly accept the high salaries and bonuses at winning; they must also accept the losses that go with the game.

However, this analysis is still too simplified. It may be well and good to argue that individual entrepreneurs ought to be allowed to fail. But, as corporations become extremely large, it is becoming increasingly difficult to allow them to fail. Competition is not so efficient after all. The consequences to society of such failure are simply too great. The Penn Central railroad was allowed to go bankrupt, but the government took over the line and established Con Rail. Lockheed and now Chrysler were not allowed to fail at all. Was it immoral for society to guarantee Chrysler loans? I think not, but I also think that we should recognize the moral implications of such loan guarantees. In a significant sense, society has now changed the rules of the game. The competition rule has been constrained by social considerations—at least for major corporations. Some companies should compete and hence do relatively better or worse with respect to each other, but competition cannot be permitted that would actually drive the losing company out of business. Some businesses are so large that society cannot afford to let them fail. In that respect society has decided that for its own protection the rule of competition as applied to major corporations in the last quarter of this century must be used less harshly. It is a bit like allowing students to receive grades A through D but without giving any failing grades.

One of the disturbing aspects of society's taming of the law of competition is that society has tamed the law only for large corporations. Small businesses and individual enterprises are allowed to fail. Why is the size of a corporation morally relevant? Is it fair to protect large corporations without protecting smaller ones? On the one hand, it seems clearly unfair. There is no relevant moral difference between large companies and small companies. Yet, on utilitarian grounds, there is a major difference. Society is benefited when competition is applied to small companies but not to large ones. Nonutilitarians are unpersuaded by such arguments, however. Unfairness, in their view, is not so easily cancelled by good consequences.

Appeal to the bankruptcy laws won't do either. On what criterion does society allow W. T. Grant to go bankrupt but not Chrysler? The appeal must once again be made to utilitarian considerations—with all the ensuing difficulties. All the bankruptcy laws do is make the consequences of the utilitarian analysis less harsh.

Anticompetitive Practices The conclusion that competition is the appropriate rule for American capitalism is much honored in theory but often denied in practice by the American business community. How did companies get to be so large? At first, they often grew by becoming a monopoly. Since monopolies are anticompetitive, both vertical and horizontal monopolies were made a violation of the antitrust laws. (Vertical monopolies occur when one company controls all the elements in the production of a product, e.g., when an oil company owns everything from the oil wells to the gasoline filling stations. Horizontal monopolies occur when a company controls all products of the same type, e.g., when all gasoline filling stations are owned by the same company.) Other noncompetitive arrangements such as cartels, interlocking directorates, and holding companies were also made illegal.

Many large corporations avoid the legal dangers involved in gaining too large a share of the market by diversification and merger. For example, an oil company could use its profits to buy airlines and hotel chains rather than additional oil companies. These mergers have become very popular, but they create ethical problems of their own. Consider the issues that the McGraw-Hill Book Company raised in fighting the American Express Company's attempt to acquire it. The following quotations from Harold McGraw's letter to the board of directors of the American Express Company illustrate some of the conflict of interest situations that did occur or could occur if the merger attempt succeeded:

> 1. One dramatic illustration of the potential for serious conflict of interest is the fact that, as a major investor in securities, American Express holds more than $3 billion in state and municipal securities and underwrites and insures additional state and municipal securities—securities that must be independently rated by McGraw-Hill's Standard & Poor's Division!
>
> 2. Mr. Roger H. Morley, President of American Express, was a director of McGraw-Hill when you formulated and made your proposal. He clearly violated his fiduciary duties to McGraw-Hill and the stockholders of McGraw-Hill by misappropriating confidential information and conspiring with American Express, the members of the Board of Directors of American Express, and others to acquire McGraw-Hill at a price, in a manner, and at a time that would be most beneficial to American Express, but to the detriment of McGraw-Hill's stockholders.
>
> 3. American Express' conspiratorial approach and lack of integrity is further emphasized by your obtaining the financing for acquisition of McGraw-Hill from Morgan Guaranty Trust Company which, for more than 50 years, has been McGraw-Hill's principal bank—a fact well known to you Mr. Morley. Any company that would use its financial power to cause a bank to violate its relationship with a client lacks the integrity and morality essential to the business of McGraw-Hill.[7]

Clearly, Mr. McGraw believes that the American Express Company has violated ethical business practice. The concept of a conflict of interest will be analyzed in Chapter 5. It is clear from the quotation, however, that diversification mergers can create situations, similar to the problems created by inside information that place individuals and firms in awkward moral situations.

However, the diversification merger, often fails on the efficiency criterion as well. Consider the following hypothetical case.

_____ **The NIL Corporation Merger** _____

NIL Corporation was a manufacturer of fasteners used in manufacturing processes. It started out as a small family-owned and -managed company, and, through dedication on the part of the owner management, NIL grew to a com-

---

[7] *The Wall Street Journal* Open letter to American Express Company from Harold McGraw of McGraw-Hill Publishers—Jan. 18, 1979.

pany with sales in excess of $100 million, profits on sales after taxes of 10 percent, and a strong balance sheet. NIL had 1,000 employees, many of whom had more than ten years of service. On the whole, they were extremely loyal to the owners and took considerable pride in turning out quality products.

To assure future financing of NIL's growth, a market was established for the company's stock by making a secondary offering of 70 percent of the owners' shares. These shares were quickly purchased and widely distributed in the over-the-counter market by the investment community. Several years after the sale of stock by the owners, the company made a primary offering of its shares, which diluted to 15 percent the 30 percent ownership of the management.

NIL's sales grew to $150 million annually largely as a result of internal growth. Everything appeared to be going well except that the owner-managers had become apprehensive about the possibility of a takeover. NIL had been approached by several conglomerate-type corporations with proposals to purchase all of NIL's capital stock. NIL's top management wanted to continue NIL's growth as an independent company and as a consequence attempted to discourage its suitors. The NIL board voted to oppose proposals made thus far on the grounds that the potential for the company's future would be interrupted. NIL consulted its attorneys and found that there were several means to attempt to prevent acquisition, but in so doing great care had to be exercised with respect to the interests of the outside shareholders. The board then submitted to shareholders at the annual meeting of NIL proposals for amending the articles of incorporation, which, when accomplished, authorized the board in arriving at a decision to consider whether any future offer that might be made for NIL's stock was in the best interest of NIL's shareholders, its employees, customers, suppliers, and the communities in which it was located. Through amendments of the bylaws, NIL would stagger its nine-member board of directors so that only three directors would be elected in any one year and require a shareholder vote of 80 percent of the shares to approve any merger that the board had voted against. All the proposals were approved by the shareholders.

Subsequently, Multi-National Corporation, with a high degree of diversification in a number of unrelated businesses, made a proposal to the NIL board to acquire all of the outstanding shares of NIL at a 35 percent premium over the current market price. The board, after careful consideration, rejected the offer on the grounds that the merger, if completed, would end the spectacular growth of NIL to the detriment of NIL shareholders, employees, customers, and suppliers and that further the several communities in which NIL had its facilities would no doubt lose NIL's local support in taxes and civic affairs.

Multi-National Corporation, faced with NIL's board rejection, made a cash tender offer directly to NIL's shareholders. NIL's board widely advertised its objection to the offer as not being in the best interests of NIL, its shareholders, employees, customers, and suppliers. With the exception of NIL's manager-owners who still held approximately 15 percent of NIL's stock, all of NIL's shareholders accepted the offer. Multi-National Corporation called a shareholders meeting of NIL at which the articles of incorporation and bylaws were amended to substantially change their original form, and a new board of directors friendly to Multi-National was elected. All the officers of NIL were removed, the NIL Corporation was liquidated, and it was reorganized as an operating division of Multi-National Corporation. The new division was named "Fastener Division."

Multi-National appointed one of its own employees as division manager.

Those in NIL's management who were known to be opposed to Multi-National were given notices of termination with severance pay based on their years of service. The name of NIL's principal product was changed to that of the Multi-National's choice, "Quik-snap." Employees at three of NIL's locations were advised that the facilities were to be closed and reopened in other states believed to foster more favorable labor conditions. Where NIL suppliers differed from those of Multi-National Corporation who could render substantially the same services, such suppliers were dropped. NIL's charitable foundation, which had been civic minded in rendering substantial support to local charities and similar activities, was reduced to giving nominal local support. The morale of the remaining employees of the new division decreased to the lowest point ever, with a number of resignations occurring throughout the managerial group.

Several years later Multi-National, disappointed with the failure of the new fastener division to meet its projections both as to growth and profitability, dismissed the manager for poor performance and sold the business and assets to a corporation interested in getting into the fastener business. The new purchaser after a period of five years has not been able to restore the fastener business to the position it had held in the fastener market when operating as the NIL Corporation.[8]

Although this case is fictitious, it is modeled after an authentic case. Indeed, in a recent *Newsweek* article on the divestiture boom,[9] companies that acquired companies are now selling off their money losers in record numbers. The case presents a clear distinction between NIL, which operated from a stakeholder broad corporate responsibility theory of the corporation, and Multi-National Corporation, which operated from a stockholder classical theory of the corporation. It is interesting to note that, whereas the NIL management treated the corporation similar to the way in which a homeowner treats his or her house, the stockholders who owned the company treated the company merely as a financial investment. The situation mirrors our discussion of property in Chapter 2. The practice of merger and divestiture raises once again most of the ethical issues raised in Chapter 2.

Should the stockholders' interests be the only ones considered? Does their "ownership" of the company make their interests predominant? Should people be removed from their positions on grounds other than merit? Should private companies be permitted to move from one community to another simply because labor conditions are better elsewhere? Our considered opinion in Chapter 2 was that the answer to most of these questions is "no." This type of merger is still relatively unregulated; there are few rules. Given our conclusions, it seems clear that there should be.

---

[8] This case was prepared by the Committee for Education in Business Ethics under a grant from the National Endowment for the Humanities.

[9] "Wall Street's New Fashion," *Newsweek*, August 25, 1980, pp. 60–61.

Finally, what about bigness per se? If a company is so successful that it captures a huge share of the market, should the company be broken up so that competition is reestablished? For example, if Chrysler were to disappear, some have argued that General Motors should be broken up into five competing separate companies: Chevrolet, Pontiac, Buick, Oldsmobile, and Cadillac. Of course, to break up General Motors in this way is to penalize General Motors for succeeding at the competitive game. With large firms, just as society cannot afford to let one firm fail, society operates on the principle that society cannot let one firm be the overwhelming winner. Given the logic of winning and losing, this result should come as no surprise. The utilitarian benefits of competition to society result from the process of competition itself, not from having actual winners and losers.

All these considerations undermine the notion that competition per se is the most efficient way to organize markets. When this conclusion is added to the conclusion that competition is not a just allocative device, from a moral point of view, the role of competition in business practice should be constrained and some of its results corrected by other social institutions.

Competition does have a role to play in business. The advantages of competition that were illustrated by the baseball analogy at the beginning of this chapter are real. Once the proper role of competition in business has been delineated, any activity that undercuts competition is illegitimate on moral grounds. Since the strongest moral argument for competition is efficiency, we can say that price fixing, monopolistic behavior, and attempts at market control are wrong. Using the language of Chapter 1, any role-related obligations that have these anticompetitive practices as their goal are not morally binding. For example, a chief executive cannot morally order his or her subordinates to engage in activities in restraint of trade. We have here another example of how role-related obligations are constrained by a "higher" moral obligation. But competition is not the be all and end all.

In other words the role of competition is primarily an instrumental one; it is certainly a partial one. Cooperation is equally important. Society cannot permit large companies to fail totally, nor can it permit a "winning" corporation to gain too great a share of the market. Finally, some areas of competition (e.g., diversified mergers) need additional rules to avoid ethically undesirable results.

Consumer Sovereignty and the Neutrality of Preferences

Yet another rule of business practice refers to the process by which business firms choose which goods and services they are to produce. According to this rule, business firms will supply what the public demands.

The consumer is king; business responds to the revealed preferences of the consumer. Data on consumers preferences are taken as given. Indeed, the fact that businesses attempt to meet consumer preferences is often used as an argument on behalf of the morality of business practices. By meeting consumer demand, business firms are contributing to the public welfare. Business practice recognizes consumer sovereignty.

Critics of capitalist business practice, however, argue that most businesspersons try to circumvent the rule that takes consumer preferences as given. Rather than respond to consumer preferences, many businesspersons try to mold or create consumer preferences. One of the most prominent champions of this view is John Kenneth Galbraith.[10] Galbraith argues that the notion of consumer sovereignty is basically a myth. If consumer preferences were taken as given, the only advertising that society would need would be strictly informational. But as every good market researcher knows, one must create and or encourage a demand for one's product. The market does not simply respond to consumers; rather, consumers respond to the market under the pressure of advertising and other forms of sales techniques.

Given human nature, the fact that business firms must often create a market for their products should come as no surprise. The necessity for demand creation can be anticipated from one of the "laws" of economic theory—specifically the law of diminishing marginal utility. Under the law of diminishing utility, a consumer's satisfaction from each additional unit of a product increases but at a decreasing rate. Stripped of its academic jargon, this simply means that a child does not enjoy the third ice cream as much as the first one. A person does not enjoy the sixth beer as much as the first. Let us apply the law of diminishing marginal utility to material goods in general. As our standard of living increases, we do not get the same satisfaction from luxuries as we do from the products that meet more basic needs. Given the desirability of increased economic growth, the so-called law of diminishing marginal utility will need to be repealed. In an affluent society, industry needs to create a demand for more goods and services. Advertising represents one means for effecting this repeal. If business really lived by the creed of consumer sovereignty, noninformational advertising would be unnecessary.

Many critics of business argue that advertising interferes with human freedom. If some advertising is coercive and undermines human freedom, it obviously undermines consumer sovereignty. What can be said about this charge that advertising coerces or unduly influences consumers and hence interferes with their free choice (consumer sovereignty)?

The philosophic tradition has distinguished two kinds of free-

---

[10] Galbraith's account as found in The Affluent Society (New York: Mentor Books, 1958), Chapters 10 and 11.

dom—negative freedom and positive freedom. Negative freedom is simply the absence of coercion or undue influence by other human beings. Most of the freedoms enumerated in the Bill of Rights are negative freedoms. They protect certain individual activities from the coercive power of agents of the state. Positive freedom, on the other hand, is a broader concept; it includes not only the absence of coercion by other human beings but also freedom from internal restraints such as ignorance and lack of ability. Positive freedom thus includes self-mastery. In this view, one cannot be genuinely free if one is under the sway of compulsive desires or is overwhelmed by depression. Nor is one free if one has no available alternatives. In summary, a person has negative freedom if he or she is not coerced or unduly influenced by others, and a person has positive freedom to do something if he or she has the ability to do that thing, has the opportunity to do it, has a genuine alternative, and is not forced by others to make the decision.

If advertising endangers freedom, it cannot pose dangers to negative freedom, since no advertiser coerces another to do something he or she does not want to do. Hence, the threat from advertising must be to positive freedom. The critics of advertising point out that some advertising diminishes genuine consumer choice. It also plays on ignorance and molds desires in such a way that one's self-mastery is undermined. Are the critics right?

The difficulty centers on the notion of self-mastery. Who is to say when a person is master of his or her fate? Either the individual decides, or the decision is made by some other authority. Suppose that, as a result of advertising, a person purchases consumer goods at the expense of an adequate savings account for the future. If the purchaser indicates that the decision represents what he or she genuinely wants to do, on what basis can an outsider deny that the decision was freely made? Suppose that one buys the toothpaste on the basis that it gives one's mouth sex appeal. One might disagree with the *reason* that the person had for buying the toothpaste, but surely the decision was free. Indeed, if ignorance is a criterion for lack of freedom, then advertising's affect on human freedom would indeed be minimal. It would only impinge on the freedom of the very ignorant. Only advertising that is deceptive would impinge on the freedom of all consumers. However, advertising in general does not undermine human freedom, and hence it is not inconsistent with consumer sovereignty.

Nonetheless, advertising may still be morally objectionable in that it influences consumers in morally inappropriate ways. What we have to do is to examine the reasons that consumers give for making the choices that they do. Under this criticism, the claim is not that consumers are not sovereign, but that consumer preferences must be morally evaluated rather than taken at face value. Advertising, it is charged, is usually not based on rational persuasion; it is usually based on nonrational persuasion. Moreover, it is charged that the nonrational persuasion appeals to our baser motives. Advertising reflects a corrupt understanding of human nature.

For example, the "Ultra-Bright gives your mouth sex appeal" ad is neither deceptive nor an intrusion on human freedom. Yet many find it unacceptable. Why? Perhaps the chief reason is that the ad is slightly indecent or slightly degrading. In that respect, the ad shares much in common with many other ads. Can the objections of the critics be summarized? I think they can.

1. Many argue that the advertising industry exploits sex. A pretty girl or a handsome guy accompanies virtually every ad, even though their presence is often not relevant to the advertising context in which the product is advertised. Often, the pretty girl is scantily clad. On some occasions, the entire ad is blatantly sexual.

2. Many argue that the advertising industry stereotypes women in subservient roles. Often, they are portrayed as dumb housewives in detergent or cleanser commercials. In medical ads, the female is the nurse, the male is the doctor.

3. Some argue that racial, religious, or other ethnic groups are shabbily treated. The "Frito Banditos" commercial aroused the ire of Mexican-Americans.

4. Still others argue that the ad emphasizes facts or situations that are irrelevant to the virtues of the product. The chief justification for advertising is the information it presents; yet many critics contend that few ads are genuinely informational.

How are such criticisms to be assessed? Matters of taste are notoriously subjective. One person's brilliant comedy routine is another's sick joke. Often, the advertiser is in a very awkward position. Nearly every ad offends someone. An advertiser can count on a number of angry letters. Let the ad be removed, however, and there will be a number of angry letters condemning the censorship of a minority that could force the withdrawal of the ad. Clearly what is needed is some rationale for deciding on the decency and dignity questions.

Once we get into matters of decency and dignity, we can expand our questions regarding the rule of consumer sovereignty even further. Not only should preferences be evaluated, but some should not be honored. Those who hold this position would not agree that business is to accept the preferences of consumers as given and that one preference is not morally superior to any other. In some cases, society at large rejects the notion that any consumer preferences (demand) should be satisfied (bring forth a product). Nearly everyone agrees that some preferences should not be acted upon. Many of the staunchest defenders of the competitive market believe that it is morally correct to refuse to produce heroin despite very great demand. Preferences for heroin are not legitimate preferences. Neither are preferences for houses of prostitution and X-rated movies—at least if those are preferences indulged in residential neighborhoods. To hold positions like these is to at least claim that some preferences are capable of moral evaluation and that political interference with some kinds of wants is justified. However, once the door is opened this far, some criterion is needed to decide which preferences are really rationally and morally desirable.

One need not use heroin and prostitution to make this point. The philosopher Peter Singer has raised the question concerning the production of meat products. In Singer's argument, society should not produce chickens, beef, and veal—at least not in the way in which they are produced now—despite the high demand for McDonald's hamburgers and Kentucky Fried Chicken. Singer's proposal is based on what he takes to be a fundamental ethical principle: Everyone is entitled to the equal consideration of his or her interests. Now certainly one objection to a system of production based on slavery is that the interests of the slaves are ignored. Singer argues that in the production of most meat products the interests of animals are ignored. The crux of Singer's analysis is his contention that there is no criterion that would allow us to take account of the suffering of humans while at the same time ignoring the suffering of animals. Since both humans and animals have the capacity to suffer, they both have an equal right to have that fact taken into consideration.

Singer then goes on to document his contention that current practices in meat production inflict great cruelty on the animals as they are raised for slaughter.

> *In order to have meat on the table at a price that people can afford, our society tolerates methods of meat production that confine sentient animals in cramped, unsuitable conditions for the entire durations of their lives. Animals are treated like machines that convert fodder into flesh, and any innovation that results in a higher "conversion ratio" is liable to be adopted. As one authority on the subject has said, "cruelty is acknowledged only when profitability ceases."* So hens are crowded four or five to a cage with a floor area of twenty inches by eighteen inches, or around the size of a single page of the New York Times. The cages have wire floors, since this reduces cleaning costs, though wire is unsuitable for the hen's feet; the floors slope, since this makes the eggs roll down for easy collection, although this makes it difficult for the hens to rest comfortably. In these conditions all the bird's natural instincts are thwarted: They cannot stretch their wings fully, walk freely, dust-bathe, scratch the ground, or build a nest. Although they have never known other conditions, observers have noticed that the birds*

vainly try to perform these actions. Frustrated at their inability to do so, they often develop what farmers call "vices," and peck each other to death. To prevent this, the beaks of young birds are often cut off.

This kind of treatment is not limited to poultry. Pigs are now also being reared in cages inside sheds. These animals are comparable to dogs in intelligence, and need a varied, stimulating environment if they are not to suffer from stress and boredom. Anyone who kept a dog in the way in which pigs are frequently kept would be liable to prosecution, in England at least, but because our interest in exploiting pigs is greater than our interest in exploiting dogs, we object to cruelty to dogs while consuming the produce of cruelty to pigs. Of the other animals, the condition of veal calves is perhaps worst of all, since these animals are so closely confined that they cannot even turn around or get up and lie down freely. In this way they do not develop unpalatable muscle. They are also made anemic and kept short of roughage, to keep their flesh pale, since white veal fetches a higher price; as a result they develop a craving for iron and roughage, and have been observed to gnaw wood off the sides of their stalls, and lick greedily at any rusty hinge that is within reach. (*Ruth Harrison, Animal Machines, Stuart, London, 1964. This book provides an eye-opening account of intensive farming methods for those unfamiliar with the subject.)[11]

Singer's account gives us pause. Perhaps consumer preferences—even widely held ones—should be subjected to moral scrutiny. Perhaps some preferences should not be honored. Many feel, however, that denying individual preferences brings dangers of its own. Milton Friedman is completely lucid on this point. He thinks that the notion of refusing to accept some individual preferences is a dangerous one. Who is to decide what preferences are proper? Certainly, we would not want government officials, or psychologists, or even philosopher-kings making that decision. Persons who want preferences denied are elitists who seek to substitute their own judgments (the voice of the few) for the democratic preferences expressed in the marketplace (the voice of the many). Such an elitist attitude toward preferences is unjustified because there are no experts on matters of value and because the "correction" of preferences is an unjust interference with consumer sovereignty. The fact that bartenders are paid more than are social workers is the price we must pay for our individual freedom.

Both Singer and Friedman have a point. On the one hand, good moral cases can be made against both gambling and the consumption of alcohol. Yet the grand experiment with Prohibition was a disastrous failure, and New Jersey has joined Nevada in legalizing casino gambling. Many states have lotteries. Obviously, many, many people wish to purchase booze and take their chances on the state lottery. Should society in-

---

[11] Peter Singer, "All Animals Are Equal," in *Ethical Theory and Business*, eds. Thomas L. Beauchamp and Norman E. Bowie (Englewood Cliffs, N.J.: Prentice-Hall, Inc., 1979), p. 418.

terfere with their choices? On the other hand, there is something sick about the alcoholic's desire for booze, the addict's desire for a fix, and even the suburban businessperson's desire for daily tranquilizers. And surely we are insensitive to the suffering of animals that we raise and slaughter to provide us meat.

Yet another consideration concerns preferences that cannot be registered in the market. The most common example are so-called public goods which were described in Chapter 2. As you recall with public goods, my consumption does not preclude your consumption. For this reason all rational consumers will understate what they are willing to pay and the "true" value of the good will not be reflected by market pricing.

The problem of registering preferences for public goods pales in comparison with the problem of registering the preferences of/for future generations. It is one of the commonly expected responsibilities of parenthood to provide for the security of your children. That is the major reason why people buy life insurance. If one is moderately wealthy, one even feels obligated to provide a trust fund that would benefit not only one's children but one's children's children and perhaps others descended even further. Such trust funds reflect a feeling of obligation to future generations.

Many would argue that, just as an individual has an obligation to his or her future descendants, society has an obligation to its. Such an obligation might be an obligation of gratitude. This generation is the beneficiary of the labors of those who came before us. We were born into a civilized society and did not have to reinvent the wheel. Now we cannot *give* the gratitude to those who benefited us, but we can *show* that gratitude by providing for the future.

But how far into the future does our obligation extend and how much of a sacrifice are we to make? On these matters there is no consensus.

Even more controversial are so-called rights of the environment. There are at least two distinct issues here. Consider the lowly snail darter that will probably become extinct as the result of dam construction in Tennessee. Some persons argue that humankind might be harmed if the snail darter becomes extinct. Most of the arguments for this position are based on arguments in biology and genetics concerning the advantages of having a wide variety of species. To the extent that these arguments have validity, the existence of the snail darter can be treated as a public good. However, recently some have argued that an entity like the snail darter has rights of its own. One who takes this position is C. D. Stone. He argues that something like the snail darter is a valuable entity in nature quite independently of nature's relation to us. Stone's chief argument for this position fits neatly into our discussion here. He argues that, unless the environment in general and natural objects within the environment are given rights, the environment will be ignored in policy disputes and in litigation among persons. One reason for making the environment itself the beneficiary of a judgment is to prevent it from being "sold out" in a negotiation among private litigants.[12]

Where has this discussion led us? First, we must conclude that the rule of consumer sovereignty, like the rule of competition, has a place in business practice, but that consumer sovereignty is neither necessary nor sufficient in ethical business practice. It is not necessary because sometimes marketing decisions should not be based on consumer preference. It is not sufficient because some legitimate preferences cannot be captured by the consumer sovereignty rule.

But what are the principles that constrain the rule? Surely we do want to avoid the elite panel of philosopher-kings or (what is more likely) the stultifying bureaucratic decision. On this point, three comments can be made. First, there is the distinction between needs and wants. A person's needs can be objectively ascertained. If one is a roofer, one needs shingles. If one has not had anything to eat all day, one is in need of food. Statements about needs are debatable. If someone says, "I need a million dollars," we can say, "No you don't. You might want a million dollars but you do not need them." The fulfillment of needs is necessary for one to maintain one's existence or to accomplish goals central to one's development as a person. Most wants are not needs in that sense. One might want escargot for dinner; one doesn't need them. In terms of preferences, whenever someone prefers the gratification of a want at the expense of a need, that preference can be criticized; the preference is not taken as given. One who puts nothing away for the future or who lives without insurance because one wants to travel to Tahiti is making a bad choice, isn't he or she? Sometimes, the preferences can be evaluated critically using the need versus want distinction.

Second, there is the standard from human nature. As you will recall, we have agreed that most advertising does not violate consumer freedom. If advertising is defective, it is defective on the basis of its appeal. It does not appeal to the higher nature of humankind; it appeals to the baser. Why use sex to sell an automobile? There is nothing wrong with sex per se, but there is something wrong in linking sexual potency, the mechanical power of an automobile, and the Trans Am. Trans Am should be sold on its own merits. By insisting on "its own merits," we are appealing to humankind's rational nature. In general we could say that one consumer preference is better than another if the preference has been considered rationally in terms of one's own rational life plan. A student who wishes to be a doctor shows poor preference ordering when in medical school he

---

[12] Christopher D. Stone, "Should Trees Have Standing? Toward Legal Rights for Natural Objects," in Beauchamp and Bowie, p. 566.

prefers evenings at the pub to studying. The full development of a theory of rational life plans lies beyond the scope of this book.

Third, we return to the device in Chapter 3—procedural justice. There is no philosophical theory that will tell us specifically which consumer preferences are legitimate and which are not. Neither is there a theory that will specify just how much of the present consumption of goods and services we should sacrifice to fulfill our obligations to future generations. The answers to these questions are decided by some procedure. In this society, however, these questions are not answered from within the practice of business; they are answered outside business in the political arena. In other words, some rules that apply to business are to be written outside business. The business game is not the only game in town. To discuss the criteria to be used in writing these rules would take us into political theory. However, the issue of government regulation will be addressed in Chapter 6. A summary is in order.

Conclusion

This chapter completes the analysis of the theoretical foundation of business ethics. In completing the analysis, we cannot claim that we have *the answer* to every problem of business ethics. Indeed in many cases the only answer is a procedural one. We have shown, however, that one's particular moral obligations in business practice are, in part, a function of the role that one plays within business. We have provided an account of the function of the corporation and have specified certain moral obligations that flow from that function. In so doing, we have shown that business practice presupposes the practice of at least a minimum morality, namely, the practice of justice and respect for legitimate individual rights. In addition, we have argued that standard business practice imposes obligations, but we have insisted that these practices be morally scrutinized. In this chapter, the practices of competition and consumer sovereignty were put under the knife. Unanswered questions were to be left to just procedures for resolution. In the next two chapters, we will examine the various procedures for getting ethical decisions made in business practice.

Self-Regulation

In previous chapters the focus was on determining the morally acceptable rules of business practice—the moral responsibilities of corporations themselves and the duties and obligations of persons working within the corporate structure. If we have done all we can do in terms of saying how businesses and businesspersons ought to behave, we have said little concerning how society can be assured that businesses and businesspersons will behave as they ought. In the remaining chapters of this book, the focus is on this latter issue.

Consider any individual who has committed himself or herself to adopting the moral point of view and who now wishes to put that perspective into practice. Such persons are faced with a distinctive problem commonly known as *weakness of will*. Individuals yield to the temptation to do what is morally wrong. The problem of weakness of will is common to all types of ethics, and hence it is a topic that deserves serious discussion in any study of business ethics.

There are two fundamental strategies for overcoming weakness of the will. One relies on internal mechanisms of self-control and the other on external constraints. These same two strategies can be adapted to the corporate setting. Internal mechanisms for self-control include business codes of ethics, changes in the decision-making process, and the corporate social audit. The chief external constraint is government regulation. In this chapter, and the next, the strengths and weaknesses of business mechanisms for self-regulation and of government regulation are discussed.

Individual Behavior Within an Institutional Setting

This chapter and the subsequent one focus on the economic institution of the business firm rather than on the individual businessperson. This focus is the result of a conscious decision concerning what society can reasonably expect concerning the moral behavior of individual businesspersons. I contend that society can expect a high level of moral behavior on the part of individual businesspersons only if the practices and reward structures of business firms support that behavior. In other words, individual ethical behavior will be impaired if such behavior either hinders or does not advance an individual's business career. If a firm expects a high level of ethical conduct, business enterprises must make sure that the moral behavior of an individual employee of that firm pays off. Hence, the discussion in this chapter is directed toward structural changes that individual firms have made or could make to enhance the probability of the individual's ethical behavior. In the course of our discussion, we will see that some of these internal mechanisms will be especially useful in providing procedural justice. Such mechanisms will be useful in resolving some of the previous indeterminacy in settling moral issues.

Codes of Business Ethics

Almost any discussion of morality eventually focuses on the desirability of basing morality on rules. Some philosophers argue that rules are central to the moral life—that morality *is* the observance of certain types of rules. Other philosophers argue that rules are simply rough guides that have some utility in morality but that there is no moral duty to follow the rules per se. This split on the role that rules are to play in the moral life extends beyond philosophy to the general public itself. On the one hand, there is a long tradition that seems to indicate that rules are central. Early in life we learn the Ten Commandments. Even today one occasionally finds articles that try to apply the Bible directly to business ethics.[1] Although it is often considered fashionable to point out that moral rules are usually stultifying and outmoded, behavioral research indicates that

---

[1] See, for example, Stanley Ford, "What the Bible Tells the Businessman," *Business Management*, Vol. 57 (December 1969), 48–51, and Reverend Billy Graham "The Answer to Corruption," *Nation's Business*, (September 1969), 46–49.

viewing morality as adherence to rules is necessary to the development of a mature morality.[2]

On the other hand, the view that moral rules are stultifying and outmoded is not without force. In some interpretations, the views of Jesus represented an ethical alternative based on love to the legal ethics of Judaism. Coincident with the social turmoil of the 1960s some philosophers and theologians popularized an antirule ethical theory known as situation ethics to replace the crumbling moral rules of that period. In periods of rapid social change, many believe that rules are not adequate as instruments for carrying the burden of morality.

It would be impossible in an introductory book on business ethics to resolve this complex debate on the status of moral rules. To facilitate the discussion of codes of business ethics, it will be assumed that moral rules are at least useful devices for assisting individuals to behave ethically. Such an assumption seems reasonably harmless given current beliefs and actions regarding moral rules. Hence, I will argue that business codes of ethics can be useful devices to assist individuals to behave ethically in the business setting. On the other hand, I certainly do not believe that moral rules are sufficient as devices to aid the individual in the practice of moral behavior, and hence I do not think that business codes of ethics are sufficient for that purpose in the business setting. In the following remarks, I will argue for these contentions, but my remarks will be limited to the use of business codes of ethics.

Advantages of Codes One advantage common to all codes of ethics is that they provide more stable permanent guides to right or wrong than do human personalities. This is the argument that Aristotle used against Plato. Plato had argued that in the ideal state decisions were to be made by the philosopher-king. The philosopher-king had special insights into the truth. There are some analogies between Plato's philosopher-king and the wise decisions of Solomon. Rules could not provide correct decisions in difficult situations; only wise good people could do that. For Plato, the achievement of ethics depends on having the right people in the right positions.

Aristotle disagreed with Plato in this respect. He argued that there were no philosopher-kings. Whereas Plato believed that, if one knew the good, one would do it, Aristotle took the notion of weakness of the will seriously. People could not be completely objective. People tend to take the short-run point of view. The passions of a situation get in the way of a wise decision. These frailties of human nature require that decisions about ethics generally be a matter of law or rules.

---

[2] Richard M. Hare, *The Language of Morals* (New York: Oxford University Press, 1964), pp. 70–78.

Over the years Aristotle's view has prevailed over Plato's, and Aristotle's position is reflected in the Anglo-American tradition. We have adopted a Constitution with a Bill of Rights that serves as a constraint not only on raw political power but also on the state's power to limit certain rights according to popular opinions as to what is right and what is wrong.

Second, codes of ethics really do provide guidance, especially in ethically ambiguous situations. In Chapter 1, I indicated that one of the difficulties with many job descriptions is that they are vague and under-determined. This is a serious fault in a situation in which what one ought or ought not to do is in large part determined by one's position (role). By tying a code of ethics to a job description, what counts as appropriate ethical conduct is clarified. Moreover, there is empirical research that supports this view that a clear set of rules does make a difference as to whether or not an employee will engage in an ethically dubious action. For example, Henry P. Sims, Jr., professor of Organizational Behavior at Penn State, has done some research with graduate students confronted with decisions-making opportunities. His results show that a clear company policy forbidding kickbacks lowers the tendency of the graduate students to permit kickbacks.[3]

Third, codes of ethics not only guide the behavior of employees, they control the autocratic power of employers. In theory at least, a business code of ethics can provide an independent ground of appeal when one is urged by an employer or supervisor to commit an unethical act. "I'm sorry, but company policy strictly forbids it" is a gracious way of ending a conversation about a "shady" deal. (Whether or not a code is sufficient for checking the autocratic demands of a superior will be discussed later.)

The three advantages cited are advantages for *all* codes of ethics, including codes of business ethics. The remaining two items apply specifically to business ethics.

A fourth advantage of codes of business ethics is that they could help specify the social responsibilities of business itself. As we saw in Chapter 4, one of the most frustrating aspects of the current debate about business ethics is that no one knows what the rules are. Most business leaders recognize that the social responsibilities of business must expand and that business executives will be held to higher ethical standards than in the past. However, there are some obvious limits. A blanket ethical demand that business solve all social problems is arbitrary and unrealistic. Business codes of ethics acceptable both to the business community and to the general public would help to bring some order out of the chaos. Later in this chapter we shall delineate what types of ethical problems are

---

[3] Henry P. Sims, "The Reinforcement of Unethical Decision Behavior: An Experiment," unpublished paper, 23 pages.

best handled by codes and what types of ethical problems are not well handled by codes.

Fifth, and perhaps most important, the development of business codes of ethics is clearly in the interest of business itself. There is virtual unanimity in the business community that unethical business practices threaten to bring about increased government regulation of business. For reasons that will be discussed in Chapter 6, government regulation of business ethics is viewed on a scale from distrust to horror. When compared with the specter of government regulation, many businesspersons agree that codes of ethics at least deserve a second look.

Codes of good business practice do serve these useful functions and are not new. After all, one of the purposes of the Better Business Bureau is to protect both the consumer and the legitimate business operator from the "fly-by-night operator." The lesson we learn from the Better Business Bureau is that business ethics is not simply in the interest of the consumer. Business ethics is in the vital interest of the business community as well. As indicated in Chapter 3, business activity depends on a high level of trust and confidence. If a firm or industry loses the confidence of the public, it will have a difficult time in selling its products. Kenneth Arrow has made this point about the medical profession.

> The fact is that if you had sufficient distrust of a doctor's services, you wouldn't buy them. Therefore the physician wants an ethical code to act as assurance to the buyer, and he certainly wants his competitors to buy this same code, partly because any violation may put him at a disadvantage but more especially because the violation will reflect on him since the buyer of the medical services may not be able to distinguish one doctor from another.[4]

Another version of the argument depends on features of decision theory, particularly a situation known as the prisoner's dilemma.[5] We can consider a variation of the prisoner's dilemma situation by considering the installation of antipollution devices. Consider the position of an executive at Bethlehem Steel who is considering whether or not Bethlehem Steel should install antipollution devices in Bethlehem Steel's plants. In making the decision, the executive must consider the position of

---

[4] Kenneth Arrow, "Social Responsibility and Economic Efficiency," *Public Policy*, Vol. 231 (Summer 1973) 314.

[5] The prisoner's dilemma (attributed to A. W. Tucker) is an illustration of a two-person noncooperative, nonzero-sum game; noncooperative because agreements are not binding (or enforceable), and nonzero sum because it is not the case that what one person gains the other loses. Thus, imagine two prisoners who are brought before the attorney general and are interrogated separately. They both know that, if neither confesses, they will receive a short sentence for a lesser offense and will spend a year in prison but that, if one confesses and turns state's evidence, he will be released, the other receiving a particularly

Bethlehem Steel in conjunction with the positions of the other steel companies. The following matrix, which is a version of "the prisoner's dilemma" situation, can illustrate the situation of Bethlehem Steel in conjunction with one of its competitors, Inland Steel.

		Bethlehem Steel	
		Invest I	Do Not Invest II
Inland Steel	Invest I	.07, .07	− .03, .10
	Do Not Invest II	.10, − .03	.04, .04

In the matrix, each of the four squares represents the payoffs to the various companies for the decision represented in the square. For example, in the square at the upper left, the payoff to both Inland Steel and to Bethlehem Steel when they both invest in the antipollution devices is a positive .07. The reader should note that in each of the squares the first number represents the payoff to Inland Steel and that the second represents the payoff to Bethlehem. (One should understand that "payoff" does not refer simply to current monetary profits; rather, it additionally includes such items as public goodwill and the positive effects of avoiding government regulations.) Now, clearly, the best result is that they both invest in antipollution devices. However, in a competitive market where each acts independently, it will be impossible to achieve the desired result (column I, row I). In the competitive situation, it will always be to Inland Steel's best interest to choose row II, no matter what Bethlehem Steel

---

heavy term of ten years; if both confess, each gets five years. In this situation, assuming mutually disinterested motivation, the most reasonable course of action for them—that neither should confess—is unstable. This can be seen from the following gain-and-loss table (with entries representing years in prison):

		Second Prisoner	
		Not confess I	Confess II
First Prisoner	Not confess I	1, 1	10, 0
	Confess II	0, 10	5,5

To protect himself, if not to try to further his own interests, each has a sufficient motive to confess, whatever the other does. Rational decisions from the point of view of each lead to a situation where both prisoners are worse off. See John Rawls, *A Theory of Justice* (Cambridge, Mass.: Harvard University Press, 1971), p. 269.

does, and it will always be to Bethlehem Steel's interest to choose column II, no matter what Inland does.

Let us illustrate this point by considering the decision procedure that would be adopted by an executive at Bethlehem Steel. Suppose that Inland Steel invests; that would place us in row I. In that row, the biggest payoff to Bethlehem is in column II. If, on the other hand, Inland Steel does not invest, then we are in row II, and once again the biggest payoff to Bethlehem in that row is column II. Hence, Bethlehem Steel should choose column II, no matter what Inland Steel does. Using a similar argument we can conclude that Inland Steel should be in row II, no matter what Bethlehem does. Hence, the conjunction of the two independent decisions will place us in the lower right-hand square (column II, row II). That square does not present the ideal payoff; rather, the square defined by column I, row I represents the best payoff.

To avoid the prisoner's dilemma situation, some means of legitimate cooperation must be permitted. In many cases, as is argued by Kenneth Arrow who uses this type of analysis, an industrywide code of ethics will provide the appropriate device for avoiding a prisoner's dilemma situation.[6] Such codes, when enforced properly, provide a means for assuring that all who subscribe to the code will behave in the morally appropriate way. In that way the firms would remain competitive with one another and would reap the benefits of morality as well. As a result of this analysis, however, it is clear that codes of ethics that apply to business firms, themselves, as distinct from those directed primarily to the actions of employees, should be industrywide. If they are not industrywide, the prisoner's dilemma situation shows that they cannot be effective.

Objections to Codes Despite the five advantages of codes of business ethics listed, codes of ethics are treated with great skepticism by many businesspersons and by representatives for the consuming public as well. What can be said against such codes?

First, there is a serious practical objection to industrywide codes of ethics. Business leaders are reluctant to sit down together to write industrywide codes in the fear that they will be in violation of the antitrust laws. My understanding of the antitrust law is that an industrywide code of ethics could be discussed under government supervision. In any case, some way should, and I am sure can, be found to permit the development of industrywide codes without violating antitrust laws.

Second, many criticize professional codes of ethics because they are too broad and amorphous. For example, consider four of the first six standards of the Public Relations Society of America.

---

[6] Arrow, "Social Responsibility," p. 314.

1. A member has a general duty of fair dealing toward his or her clients or employees, past and present, his or her fellow members, and the general public.

2. A member shall conduct his or her professional life in accord with the public welfare

3. A member has the affirmative duty of adhering to generally accepted standards of accuracy, truth, and good taste.

4.

5.

6. A member shall not engage in any practice that tends to corrupt the integrity of channels of public communication.

By using such terms as "fair dealing," "public welfare," "generally accepted standards," and "corrupt the integrity," the code of standards of the PRSA could be charged with being too broad and amorphous.

To adequately assess this criticism, a few comments about the nature of language are in order. Except in the use of proper names, language is always general and is always in need of interpretation. Consider a municipal law: "No vehicles are allowed in the park." What counts as a vehicle? a bicycle? a skateboard? a baby carriage? Moreover, whenever we have a definition, there are certain borderline cases. When is a person bald or middle aged? I used to think that thirty-five was middle aged. Now I am not so sure. The point of these comments is to show that some of the criticisms of business codes are usually not criticisms of the code but of the language itself. This generality of the criticism provides the clue for mitigating the problem. After all, the institution known as the law is a well-entrenched social institution, and it is an institution that is based heavily in language. So, after all, is business practice. Contracts, collective bargaining agreements, warranties, and the like are all linguistic devices that facilitate the practice of business. If language usage is as broad and amorphous as the critics contend, what accounts for the operational success of law and business?

I submit that the answer to this question is twofold. First language is not so broad and amorphous after all. The terms of a language have what H. L. A. Hart refers to as a "settled core of meaning."[7]

Consider the rule that forbids vehicles to enter the park. Clearly, there are some borderline cases—roller skates, a baby carriage. But there are clear cases as well. Automobiles are to be forbidden. If one accepts the notion of a settled core of meaning, then most uses of a word are clear

---

[7] H. L. A. Hart, *The Concept of Law* (New York: Oxford University Press, 1961), pp. 124–141.

enough. It is only at the borderline where controversies concerning application develop. The message for those constructing codes of business ethics seems quite clear. If the code is constructed with the settled core of meaning of the words in mind, ambiguity will be cut to a minimum. If the code of ethics is taken seriously, the choice of words will be taken seriously as well.

Admittedly, however, ambiguities and insufficiencies will remain. The code will still need interpretation, and hence procedures must be adopted for interpreting what the code means and what the code requires. However, this is no more of a problem for a code of business ethics than it is for other uses of language. The law itself, even at the highest level represented by the Constitution, requires a Supreme Court to make a final decisive interpretation. Even now in certain situations, the courts must interpret what a warranty or a collective bargaining agreement means. When an impasse on a warranty develops, a court proceeding will make the final determination as to what the warranty says. Although frequently the law is the social institution most often appealed to when disagreements concerning the terms of a contract arise, other possibilities arise. The Better Business Bureau has an appeal procedure that can culminate in binding arbitration. Moreover, this provision for binding arbitration is used frequently. Perhaps the Better Business Bureau or some professional association might serve as an independent body for making the final interpretation as to what a code of ethics means and for determining when it applies and when it does not.

Discussions concerning the interpretation of a code of ethics lead naturally to the third most common criticism of business codes of ethics— they are not adequately enforced. I concur that a code of ethics without adequate enforcement is hardly a code at all. An effective code of ethics must be enforced and must have real penalties attached to it to punish disobedience. Of course, simply having the penalties on the books is not enough. In a home where discipline is taken seriously, a certain atmosphere pervades. I submit that, in a company where ethics is taken seriously, a certain atmosphere will also pervade. Since I do not work in a business corporation, I cannot identify all the signs that indicate that the right atmosphere exists, but I can mention some possibilities discussed in the literature.

First, the business would *not* have as its guide on ethical matters the principle "If it is not illegal, it is not unethical." Such an attitude is not appropriate because at most the law prescribes minimum standards of ethical behavior. However, many of the serious problems in business ethics lie outside the law. An illustration should enable us to establish the first point. We have previously seen that one of the important issues in business ethics is employee rights, particularly the right of an employee to refuse to obey an immoral order without being fired. The law on this issue provides no such extensive right. However, morality requires that, in the practice of business, such a right be taken seriously. The business that limits its ethics to legality has an extremely limited ethics.

Moreover, the attitude "if it's not illegal, it's ethical" is ultimately self-defeating. By depending upon the law, one is encouraging the government regulations to which most businesspersons strongly object. The American Institute for Certified Public Accountants recognizes this point when it describes its code of professional ethics as a voluntary assumption of self-discipline above and beyond the requirements of law.

Second, I would expect some demonstration on the part of management that the code will be enforced effectively. Employees are perfectly aware of productivity goals, and a manager who misses the goal is penalized. Since it is a fact about much business practice that there is little penalty for bad ethical decisions but often severe penalties for failure to meet sales or profit goals, there is a built-in pressure for unethical behavior. In fact, some people in business believe that the most serious obstacle to business ethics is this internal pressure to improve the bottom line. Every low-level manager and supervisor recognizes the consequences for behavior expressed in the following syllogism.

1. If a code of ethics is really to be taken seriously, management must give it the same status as directives that affect profits.

2. Management does not give codes of ethics the same status as directives that affect profits.

3. Therefore, management is not really serious about its codes of ethics.

If codes of ethics are to work, they must be enforced and the most important step in getting them enforced is to get them taken seriously by the management. How is that to be done? Phillip T. Drotning of Standard Oil of Indiana puts it this way:

> *Several generations of corporate history have demonstrated that any significant corporate activity must be locked into the mainstream of corporate operations or it doesn't get done. Social policies will remain placebos for the tortured executive conscience until they are implemented with the same iron fisted management tools that are routinely employed in other areas of activity to measure performance, secure accountability, and distribute penalties and rewards.*[8]

---

[8] Phillip T. Drotning, "Organizing the Company for Social Action," in *The Unstable Ground: Corporate Social Policy*, S. Prakash Sethi (Los Angeles: Melville Publishing Co., 1974), p. 259.

Exhortations are not enough, however. Someone in the corporation should be responsible for ensuring that all employees of the company subscribe to high ethical standards. Many suggestions for institutionalizing this concern with ethics have been mentioned, and some have been implemented. Theodore Purcell has advocated electing an "angel's advocate" to the board of directors. This person would be an expert in matters of business ethics, and it would be his or her responsibility to make sure that the ethical perspective be brought to bear on all major corporate decisions.

> *We should institutionalize ethical expertise at the board of directors and top-management levels, focusing on one director but with responsibilities shared by a committee of the board. This director/ethical advocate need not be a philosopher in the field of ethics, but he should keep up to date on the extensive literature of ethics as applied to business.*
>
> *A principal function of the ethical office would be to identify generic questions of an ethical nature that should be asked routinely along with the usual legal, financial, and marketing questions. For example: A strategic planner might ask, "If we take certain actions, what would our market share be, and will we run afoul of antitrust laws?" The ethics advocate might want to know how a given decision will affect the rights of employees versus the rights of the corporation. Or, will an action help or hurt the long-run general welfare of the cities or countries (South Africa, for instance) where plants are located?*
>
> *The corporate ethics advocate would need to be socially sensitive enough to phrase such questions in generic terms, but still keep them sufficiently practical and thus manageable for specific top management decisions. It would be up to this director to cooperate where necessary with ethics officers from other firms. He might help develop an ethical code for the company and could encourage ethics seminars for top, middle and lower managers in their midcareers when their experience will lead them to see more clearly the ethical implications of their decisions.*
>
> *All this calls for an ethics director who is a strong and able manager and who has the backing of his chief executive officer.*[9]

Purcell's idea has been adopted by some companies. Perhaps the best known "angel's advocate" is Leon Sullivan, pastor of the Zion Baptist Church of Philadelphia and the first black director of the General Motors Corporation. Sullivan speaks of himself as a public interest director—a position that he defines in the following way:

> *When I speak of the public interest director, I mean an individual who takes up a position on a corporate board with specific intent to represent, at least initially and directly, other interests than those of the shareholders who own*

---

[9] Theodore Purcell, "Electing an Angel's Advocate to the Board," *Management Review*, Vol. 65 (May 1976), 9–10.

the business. I mean, to give a specific example, a black who comes on a corporate board with the clearly understood mission of getting more equitable treatment for blacks and members of other minorities throughout the business.[10]

Although Sullivan was initially skeptical about taking this position, he wrote enthusiastically about his experience. Some explanation for his enthusiasm focuses on the results. When he started with General Motors in 1970, there were seven black directors; by 1974 there were twenty. In thirty months, there were five thousand advancements of blacks to salaried positions. Few black businesses were supplying General Motors with products, but in 1974 more than four hundred black suppliers had $20 million in annual contracts. General Motors wrote more than $1.5 billion in insurance business with black insurance companies; two years earlier General Motors had written zero.

Speaking of pollution, Sullivan assessed the situation as follows:

Prior to my coming on the board, I was of the opinion that these men had a limited concern about matters such as pollution. I was wrong. Indeed, more than half of the board meetings were spent in dealing with questions of public concern and I found that hundreds of millions of dollars were being expended in the utilization of the best scientific and technical knowledge available to deal with problems of ecology, pollution, and emission. Of course, this is necessary for an automobile company, because the solution to pollution problems is, in today's climate, related to the survival of the automobile industry. It was interesting to note the degree to which I found this and a mounting interest in human needs and community problems among directors of General Motors.

General Motors is not doing all that it should do, and is not yet doing all that it could do, but it certainly is doing a lot better than it used to do; and you can be sure I will strive to see that they keep on doing more, because I will certainly keep on talking and doing my best to push the company along in these directions.[11]

Despite Sullivan's endorsement based on experience, the number of companies placing public interest members on their boards has not grown significantly in the past few years. John Steiner has identified five common objections to public interest directors. First, there is the danger that business executives might confuse their economic mission with altruistic

---

[10] Leon H. Sullivan, "Problems and Opportunities of Public Interest Directors" in *Managing the Socially Responsible Corporation,* ed. Melvin Anshen, (New York: Macmillan Publishing Co., Inc., 1974), pp. 169–170.

[11] Ibid., p. 174.

concerns. Second, since ethical problems cannot be precisely defined or quantified, it would be difficult to develop standards for making ethical decisions. Third, the methods of ethical advisors are antithetical to business management techniques. Fourth, if the ethical specialists had both perfectionist moral standards and power, they could tyrannize a business organization. Fifth, the supply of qualified advisors on matters of ethics is woefully short.[12]

Some of these objections are of a practical nature and are capable of a practical resolution. Others, especially numbers 1 and 3, are really ideological. Both objections reflect a common viewpoint, namely, that business and ethics are incompatible both in outlook and in method. The argument of this entire book can be seen as an extended critique of that position.

Another objection to public interest directors was not mentioned by Steiner. By institutionalizing matters of ethics in one person, the rest of the company employees are "off the hook." The public interest director becomes *the* ethics person; everyone else can direct his or her attention to the more important work of increasing profits. If such an attitude should in fact develop, the very purpose of having a public interest director will be thwarted. Instead of increasing the awareness of ethical issues, the public interest director would actually decrease such awareness. If factual evidence indicated that this criticism was correct, at the very least the public interest director would need additional institutional support. Otherwise, this attempt at self-regulation would not be effective.

Some have argued that a more radical approach must be taken. The *entire* corporate decision-making process must be constrained so that ethical decisions are more likely to be made. One suggestion made by Christopher Stone is that of legally requiring the company to establish structures so that certain moral judgments do in fact get made. Stone cites some examples of what he has in mind:

1. Current regulations of the Food and Drug Administration that require the establishment of quality control units whose powers and responsibilities are set by government authorities.
2. Criteria that set qualifications as to who may and who may not hold certain corporate positions.
3. Federal Communications Commission regulations that insist that

---

[12] John F. Steiner, "The Prospect of Ethical Advisors for Business Corporations," in *Issues in Business and Society,* eds. George A. and John F. Steiner, 2nd ed. (New York: Random House, Inc., 1972), pp. 284–286.

someone in authority know the lyrics of the records played on the air.

4. National Institute of Mental Health guidelines for genetic research.

Stone maintains that his approach represents an innovation that will raise the level of corporate conduct.

> All these forms of control can be classified as what I call "organizational adjustment measures." Unlike the traditional approaches, their focus is not so much on what organizations do, but on the ways organizations decide.[13]

Just how far corporations ought to move on their own toward institutional adjustments is a matter of controversy. At the very least I would recommend that a high-level officer, presumably a vice president, with suitable staff support should be empowered to interpret and enforce the business code of ethics. This vice president should have the same status as the vice president for marketing, production, personnel, and so on. The vice president should also be responsible for measuring performance.

Now it must be admitted that this response to the criticism that codes of ethics are not adequately enforced is a concession to Plato in his argument with Aristotle. Codes of ethics by themselves are not sufficient devices to provide the climate for a desirable record on business ethics. Codes of ethics must be buttressed by internal mechanisms within the corporation if they are to be effective. They must be interpreted adequately and enforced effectively by ethical persons. Ethics is not simply a matter of good laws. Nor is ethics simply a matter of having good people. If the ethical perspective is to be effective in human behavior, both good laws and good people are necessary. Both the Platonic and the Aristotelian insights are necessary.

This discussion should represent the answer to a common criticism of codes of business ethics, namely, that they are mere window dressing—public relations gimmicks, if you will. Of course many are that. The philosophical question is whether or not there is something in the logic of codes of ethics that requires them to be nothing more than public relations gimmicks. I submit that codes need not be doomed to public relations stunts. Consider codes for the employees within a company. If these codes are well written, have an official body for interpretation and application, and are adequately enforced, they do represent an effective means for obtaining ethical behavior.

When we focus on codes that affect industrywide practices and hence can only be effective if they are adopted by all the competitors in a

---

[13] Christopher D. Stone, "Controlling Corporate Misconduct," *The Public Interest*, Vol. 48, (Summer 1977), 67.

given industry, we have an effective test for determining whether or not that type of code is a public relations gimmick. Since any code not adopted industrywide would place the company at a competitive disadvantage, we can be fairly certain that a company code that addresses industrywide practices but that is not adopted industrywide probably is nothing but window dressing. On the other hand, as the "prisoner's dilemma" illustration (page 94) indicates, an industrywide code based on rational self-interest would be in the interest of each individual company. An industrywide code is designed to protect legitimate businesses from the unethical acts of competitors. They are also designed to preserve the trust and confidence of the public that is necessary for the survival of the industry itself. Hence, such codes are not mere window dressing but, rather, are enlightened investments to be made by successful corporate enterprises.

Codes of Business Ethics and Multinationals The recent growth of interest in business ethics can be traced in part to the revelations concerning bribes made by multinational corporations to officials of foreign governments to obtain lucrative contracts. Actually, the existence of multinational corporations creates many problems of business ethics. At this point, it would be useful to cite some of the ethical dilemmas that can occur in the business practices of multinationals as examples of instances in which business codes of ethics might be applied usefully and in which the use of business codes of ethics would not be helpful in resolving the issues. To accomplish this goal, a distinction must be drawn between a conflict of interest and competing interests.[14]

A conflict of interest is a collision of interests whereby the resolution of the conflict requires that only one of the interests be met and that all other interests in the conflict must yield and not be fulfilled at all. Competing interests, on the other hand, represent legitimate interests that cannot be fulfilled and in which resolution of the conflict permits a balancing of the interests so that all the interests could be partially fulfilled. "Where competing interests obtain, an unfortunate agent is somehow bound to act properly in accord with both; where a conflict of interest obtains, he must not undertake the relevant ventures conjointly; he must divest himself of at least one."[15] If all this seems unnecessarily abstract, perhaps an example will clear things up. Let us begin with a domestic issue in product safety.

---

[14] This analysis was taken from Joseph Margolis, "Conflicts of Interest and Conflicting Interests" in *Ethical Theory and Business*, eds. Thomas Beauchamp and Norman Bowie, (Englewood Cliffs, N.J.: Prentice-Hall, Inc., 1979), pp. 361–372. Whereas he used the term "conflicting interests," I am using the term "competing interests" (at the suggestion of a reviewer).

[15] Ibid., p. 363.

A Conflict of Interest

Company X discovers that one of its products has serious harmful side effects, whereas the competing product produced by another company apparently does not. Should company X stop production on this profitable product?

A Case of Competing Interests

Company X produces an artificial sweetener that has great health value to diabetics and overall health benefits to Americans suffering from overweight. However, there is some evidence that the artificial sweetener will cause a small number of persons to contract cancer. There is no available substitute. In the absence of laws governing the case, should company X stop producing the artificial sweetner?

Using our distinction between competing interests and a conflict of interest, we can give a very different analysis of the two cases. Case 1 presents a genuine conflict of interest—the interest of company X in marketing a profitable product and the interest of consumers in not having their health endangered. In this case, there is no balancing to be done; the health of the consumers is to take precedence over the interest of the company. The rationale for this is provided by the argument that no corporation should impose a clearly avoidable harm on consumers. In this case, if consumers use the competitive product, no consumers are harmed. Preventing health hazards has a higher moral priority than the profits of an individual company. With this particular product, the interest of company X is not to count at all.

Case 2 is very different, however. We are not simply balancing off the profits of company X against the harm to consumers. Rather, we are balancing off the harm to some consumers if the artificial sweetener is produced against the harm to other consumers if the artificial sweetener is not produced. In this case, we have competing interests in which the notions of weighing and balancing are much more in order. In this case, it is not obvious which interest should predominate.

This distinction is useful as an aid for determining what role codes of business ethics might serve in the international arena. It is my contention that codes of business ethics have no utility when the problem is one of competing interests but that they might be of considerable use when the problem is one of a conflict of interest. In cases of competing interests, by hypothesis all the interests in the conflict are legitimate. It is not the case that one interest is to predominate and hence all the other interests are to yield. In these cases, there must be a balancing of interests. The person responsible for the balancing must have skills in judgment and management; an appeal to a code will not do in situations such as that. To ensure that such decisions are made ethically, the notion of procedural justice discussed in Chapter 3 will serve our purposes. Since cases involving conflicts of interest admit to no one correct answer, morality requires that the decision be made according to procedural rules and from the moral point of view.

In conflict of interest cases, however, codes do play a definite role. Since, in conflict of interest cases, one interest must yield to another, codes can set such priorities. The Caterpillar Tractor Company has actually adopted an international code that announces Caterpillar's policy on some conflict of interest situations. Here are some examples:

> *Other things being equal, facilities will give preference to local sources of supply, and to local candidates for employment and promotion*
>
> *We aspire to a single standard of fair treatment of employees . . .*
>
> *Wherever in the world Caterpillar products are manufactured, they will be of uniform design and quality. Wherever possible, parts and components are to be identical.*
>
> *We don't buy unneeded materials or currencies for the holding of them for speculative resale.*
>
> *Prices are not to be influenced by superficial differences in taxation between countries.*[16]

Note the number of conflict of interest situations addressed by the Caterpillar code. Does Caterpillar use local sources of supply and local employees, does it shop around for the cheapest, or does it use American supplies and employees? The commitment is to the former. Does one use host standards for the treatment of employees or does one appeal to a universal moral standard? One adopts the universal moral standard of fair treatment. Will Caterpillar speculate on currency or adopt a pricing policy responsive to superficial differences in taxation? No. In each of these cases, one interest yields completely to another, and the code specifies which interest is to yield to the other. As illustrated, codes of ethics can indicate areas in which the scramble for increased profits would not be permitted. With respect to conflicts of interest, codes of international business ethics help to provide the rules of the game. Their function is extremely important in the absence of a world government or even multinational business and trade agreements.

It is interesting to see how historical circumstances fit with both the

---

[16] "A Code of Worldwide Business Conduct," in *The Corporate Social Challenge: Cases and Commentaries*, eds. Frederick D. Sturdivant and Larry N. Robinson, (Homewood, Ill.: Richard D. Irwin, Inc., 1977), pp. 321–328.

theoretical analysis here and with some of the theoretical analyses presented in this book. The disclosures in the mid-1970s of corporate bribery at the international level and of illegal political contributions at the national level elicited an intense demand for new federal legislation. In December 1977, the Foreign Corrupt Practices Act of 1977 was passed. The act makes it a criminal offense to bribe any high government official to obtain or retain business. Since this act applied to U.S. corporations, the U.S. business community argued that they were put at an unfair competitive disadvantage. Recall the game theory analysis of industrywide codes of ethics presented earlier in this chapter. Partly as a result of the growing pressures for a federal statute, the U.S. business community supported attempts to reach international agreements on the questionable payments issue. A step in this direction occurred with the approval by the Organization for Economic Cooperation and Development of a set of guidelines for multinational enterprises.

These guidelines were rather specific, and it would not be inappropriate to refer to them as a code of ethics. Unfortunately, the guidelines cannot be enforced and hence lack one of the essential characteristics of an effective code of ethics. However, there is sufficient institutional structure to revise the guidelines and to place some moral pressure on multinationals that do not observe them. The International Chamber of Commerce also approved a set of guidelines governing questionable payments. These standards, like their OECD counterparts, lacked adequate enforcement provisions. Finally, a United Nations agency (ECOSOC) has been working on a multilateral treaty that would embody a comprehensive code of conduct for multinational corporations.

In summary, bribery by multinationals has been recognized as an ethical problem for which a code or rules of conduct is the appropriate remedy. However, it is also recognized that the code or rule must apply transnationally if it is not to put the multinationals of the United States at a competitive disadvantage. To this extent, theory and practice coincide.

The Corporate Social Audit

Much philosophical writing in ethics is directed toward theories of what one ought or ought not to do. Very little philosophical writing focuses on how people can be moral even when they know what they ought or ought not to do. No philosophical writing is directed toward measuring how successful we are at doing what we ought to do. A business executive concerned with business ethics is not likely to omit the measurement of success. After all, the business executive is trained to focus on the traditional measure of success or failure—profits.

The yearly financial report provides data on the financial health of the corporation, and the statement of profit provides a measure of its success. As corporations respond to the demand for greater social responsibility, it is not surprising that corporate executives would be interested in measuring their success. Using the yearly financial report, which is prepared on the basis of a financial audit as a model, several persons initially suggested that a similar audit and accompanying social responsibility report be undertaken. In this way a corporation's success in ethical behavior could be measured in roughly the same way that a company's financial success is measured. On the basis of this reasoning the corporate social audit was born. The notion of the corporate social audit was sufficiently intriguing that the Committee for Economic Development commissioned a study by John Corson and George Steiner. The results of their study were published in 1974. The rationale provided for a social audit coheres very well with the thesis of this book.

> Society in America and elsewhere grants the corporation the right to exist. By issuing a corporate charter, it endows the corporation with certain privileges . . . and many unspecified but valuable rights. . . . In return for these and other legal privileges and rights society expects certain standards of behavior. . . . In the intervening years society has vastly increased its expectations. . . . It follows from this that the corporation will be called upon, formally or by the subtle pressures of public opinion, to make known how it is measuring up to its responsibilities. Thus the social audit flows logically from the social contract and from the expectation rooted in this contract.[17]

Once a consensus is reached that we ought to measure corporate success in the ethical arena, the consensus dissolves when the discussion turns to what should be measured. Some argue that the "audit" should consist of both an "asset" and "liability" account. The asset account would reflect the items that the corporation ought to have done and did. The liability account would reflect those items that the corporation ought not to have done and did as well as those items the corporation ought to have done, but did not. The asset side would also include beneficial actions that the corporation performed that were neither legally nor morally required. In other words, the asset side of the ledger would list obligations successfully performed and supererogatory acts; the debit side would list obligations violated and obligations not performed.

But what are the obligations of a corporation that should be listed? The CED report has three distinct categories:[18] (1) statutorily required activities, (2) voluntary activities, and (3) socially useful activities undertaken for profit. There is some debate, however, as to whether categories 1 and 3 should be included. With regard to statute requirements, it can be

---

[17] John J. Corson and George Steiner in collaboration with Robert C. Meehan, *Measuring Business's Social Performance: The Corporate Social Audit* (New York: Committee for Economic Development, 1974), pp. 43–44.

[18] Ibid., p. 46.

argued that corporations obey the law in their own self-interest—that obedience to law is part of the "price" that a company must pay for being permitted to play the game. Just as we do not normally praise a baseball team for moral behavior in following the rules of the game, neither should we heap moral praise on businesses for following the rules of the business game. A similar analysis can be applied to category 3. Profits are in the interest of the corporation. It may well be that society should try to find ways to make morality pay in terms of profit. That would certainly make it easier for a corporation to behave morally. However, a corporation deserves no special moral credit for acting in its enlightened self-interest.

I suggest a different solution to the question of what should be measured by a corporate social audit. I suggest that that question be settled by appealing to the neoclassical definition of the proper function of a corporation. That account indicates that the function of a corporation is to seek reasonable profits consistent with the canons of justice and with respect for individual rights. Since this neoclassical definition represents the minimally acceptable definition of the function of a corporation, an adequate account must at least measure success in these three areas: justice, respect for rights, and profit. The reasonable profit criterion is already handled adequately by the traditional financial audit.

With respect to the other two items of justice and rights, a corporation should record on the debit side any actions that violate either the canons of justice or respect for individual rights. In this way, obligations violated would appear.

On the asset side would be the cost to the company of avoiding harm and of providing for individual rights. It may seem strange to enter costs on the asset side. Remember, however, that we are providing an ethical balance sheet. Doing the right thing often does cost, but doing the right thing surely belongs on the asset side of an ethical balance sheet.

What would a social audit constructed according to these principles show? It would show the moral cost for that company in making the profits it did. A picture of what profit at what cost would be very useful to society and particularly to any investor who took morality as seriously as profits. It would also provide another institutional means for providing corporate executives with a measure of the costs of achieving a certain level of profit. Executives would not only compare financial balance sheets; they would also compare ethical cost sheets as well. Competition would not be solely for highest profits, but rather it would be for highest profits consistent with the least moral cost.

Many corporations, as we saw in Chapter 2, find the neoclassical definition of the function of the corporation to be too narrow. The executives of those corporations wish to do more than adhere to the canons of justice and to respect individual rights. They wish to take positive steps on behalf of the public good. Philosophers classify actions of the latter type as acts that are morally good but are not morally required. Sometimes actions of this type are referred to as supererogatory acts. Since these acts are not morally required, but yield morally good results, they should be recorded on the asset side of the ledger. Hence, a complete social audit would include the traditional financial statement, a liability statement showing moral costs of doing business, and an asset statement showing the financial cost of doing supererogatory moral acts. In this way the full relation between morality and profit will be publicly visible.

Suppose that we accept this description of the appropriate contents of a corporate social audit. Our problems are not yet at an end. An agreement on *what* to count does not automatically create an agreement on *how much* to count it. Consider a few simple situations. Suppose a corporation finds that a competitor has improved its product so that the competing product is clearly superior. The corporation improves its research and development, but none of that will help in the short run. In the short run, the advertising budget is raised drastically, and the taste and accuracy of the ads clearly decline. A few employees complain about these tactics and are unequivocally informed to keep quiet or lose their jobs. By engaging in such short-run practices, the corporation maintains profits. The financial balance sheet looks as good this year as it did last year. However, the profit margins have been retained at additional moral costs. But how should these moral costs be quantified? What numbers should appear in the liability column?

To further complicate our example, suppose that this same corporation that has incurred these short-run moral costs to stay competitive has an exemplary record in terms of supererogatory acts. The corporation has invested heavily in the inner city, has gone the extra mile on hiring minorities and women, and has provided free counseling and psychological care for employees suffering emotional problems including alcoholism and drug abuse. Surely these activities should be entered in the asset column. Moreover, we should compare assets and liabilities to get a true picture of the moral nature of this corporation. But, even more important, we want to compare this corporation with others.

Despair at arriving at any numbers might lead one to give up the attempt at quantification. Perhaps, such persons might argue, a verbal reporting of the moral costs is enough. Some executives have urged that the CPA accounting model be given up for something less precise. Such a response will probably not do. How could an accurate comparison be done on the basis of verbal reports alone? Verbal reports just will not give us what we want. However, if we need quantitative measures, how can they be achieved? Most experts agree that suitable measures do not now exist. Here is a sample of the opinion:

XXXX Corporation
Socio economic Operating Statement for the Year Ending December 31, 1971

I Relations with People

A. Improvements

1. Training program for handi-capped workers — $10,000
2. Contribution to educational institution — 4,000
3. Extra turnover costs because of minority hiring program — 5,000
4. Cost of nursery school for children of employees, voluntarily set up — 11,000

   Total improvements — $30,000

B. Less: Detriments

1. Postponed installing new safety devices on cutting machines (cost of the devices) — 14,000

C. Net improvements in people actions for the year — $16,000

B. Less: Detriments

1. Cost that would have been incurred to relandscape strip mining site used this year — $ 80,000
2. Estimated costs to have installed purification process to neutralize poisonous liquid being dumped into stream — 100,000

   180,000

C. Net deficit in Environment actions for the year — $(97,000)

III Relations with Product

A. Improvements

1. Salary of V.P. while serving on government Product Safety Commission — $ 25,000
2. Cost of substituting lead-free paint for previously used poisonous lead paint — 9,000

   Total improvements — $ 34,000

II Relations with Environment
A. Improvements
1. Cost of reclaiming and landscaping old dump on company property ... $70,000
2. Cost of installing pollution control devices on plant A smokestacks ... 4,000
3. Cost of detoxifying waste from finishing process this year ... 9,000
   Total improvements ... $83,000

B. Less: Detriments
1. Safety device recommended by Safety Council but not added to product ... 22,000

C. Net Improvements in product actions for the year ... $12,000

Total Socio economic deficit for the year ... $(69,000)

Add: Net cumulative socio economic Improvements as at January 1, 1971 ... 249,000
Total net socio economic actions to December 31, 1971 ... $180,000

Source: David F. Linowes, "An Approach to Socio-Economic Accounting," *Conference Board RECORD*, November 1972, p. 60. © The Conference Board. Used by permission.

> *social auditors need generally accepted social standards against which to measure, but these standards frequently do not exist, or data that do exist may not be usable to reach any kind of consensus on social criteria.*[19]
>
> *The development of the social audit today is hobbled . . . by confusion of purpose as well as by difficulties confronted in striving to measure costs and accomplishments.*[20]

Despite these difficulties, corporate social audits are being done and many of them attempt to quantify the moral data. Two of the more thorough audits have been made by David Linowes and Clark Abt. Examine the Linowes example following. Among other things, notice that the Linowes example conforms rather well to the theoretical structure outlined earlier.

Even if the attempts by Linowes, Abt, and others bear fruit, our problems with measurement are not yet at an end. As long as *each* company performs its own social audit, other companies and the general public will treat the audit with considerable suspicion. A company-prepared social audit will always suffer from a cloud of suspicion. Corporate social audits will only be taken seriously when they are either prepared or verified by independent social auditing firms. What is being recommended is that corporate social audits be treated analogously with corporate financial audits. Professional accounting firms do financial audits. Either professional accountants or a new profession could serve as social accountants. There is no theoretical reason why business should reject the conventional professional rules of social accountants. What is needed is an accepted body of conventions for making the measurements. What troubles most business executives, I suspect, is the fact that, while they are quite familiar with the conventions of financial accounting, they are apprehensive about living with a new and very different set of conventions for social accounting. Business executives are apprehensive about being evaluated on new grounds. Their apprehension in this regard is quite understandable. Nonetheless, there is no philosophical reason why the pioneering efforts of Linowes, Abt, and others cannot be formulated into a set of professional social accounting standards. Moreover, so long as business both takes social responsibility seriously and remains committed to measuring successes and failures, the corporate social audit should not be allowed to die—at least not until a superior measure is developed.

---

[19] David H. Blake, William C. Frederick, and Mildred S. Myers, *Social Auditing: Evaluating the Impact of Corporate Programs* (New York: Praeger Publishers, 1976), p. 42.

[20] Corson et al., *Measuring Business's Social Performance*, p. 49.

Conclusion

In this chapter we have examined various attempts at corporate self-regulation. The key to self-regulation is a management team committed to maintaining a high standard of ethical behavior. Their efforts will be aided by a well-formulated code of business ethics, and their success will be measured by an independent corporate social audit. The likelihood of success will be increased as the corporation makes adjustments in the corporate structure and its decision-making procedures that allow the ethical ramifications of corporate action to receive more attention.

Nonetheless, just as individual self-regulation often proves inadequate, so does business self-regulation. To offset such failures, government regulation is viewed as either an appropriate supplement or an appropriate alternative.

Government Regulation

The most obvious alternative to the self-regulation of business is government regulation. Indeed government regulation is both widely used and widely criticized. In this chapter, we will consider some of the advantages, disadvantages, and limitations of government regulations as a means for ensuring acceptable ethical behavior on the part of business.

Before discussing government regulation per se, it is worth pointing out that business practice presupposes an effective government. As we have seen, business activity would not take place in a society where certain moral practices were not operative; business activity requires a minimally just society. It is one of the tasks of government to enforce this moral minimum—to provide for law and order. We have also seen that business is a rule-governed activity. When disputes arise *within* business as to what the rules require, for example, what is or is not entailed by a given contract, it is the function of government to serve as an umpire for interpreting the rules. The judiciary is the branch of government where businesspersons who disagree about the terms of a contract can get their disputes resolved. It is also that branch of government to which a businessperson can turn to get a contract enforced against an unwilling contractee. Leaving aside legislation that is designed specifically to support business, government serves business in two important ways: It enforces and sustains the minimum social morality that makes business possible. It also interprets and enforces the rules of business activity. Except for anarchists, even persons holding the most conservative positions on the scope of government authority agree that capitalism requires a government with sufficient authority and power to maintain a minimum sense of justice, to enforce business contracts, and to serve as an umpire to interpret the rules of the business game. Business activity is not any more possible in an ungoverned society than it is in an unjust society.

Advantages of Government Regulation

In Chapter 4, we analyzed the important role that competition played in business practice. Competition is one of the rules of business practice, and the first instances of government regulation grew out of the unanimously recognized authority of government to interpret and enforce the rules of competition. In its initial phase, government regulation was designed to protect both business and the public from anticompetitive practices. This protection included the regulation of natural monopolies (e.g., the utilities or telephone companies). In industries like these, it makes no sense to have competing companies. Imagine three different phone companies serving the same area. Later this anticompetitive regulatory task was expanded to protect the public from unfair competitive practices as well. Government regulation expanded to focus on fraud, deception, and dishonesty. In this latter sphere, the public is perhaps most familiar with the government regulation of deceptive advertising by the Federal Trade Commission.

It is important to emphasize that this type of government regulation—when conducted fairly and efficiently—both ought to be and in fact is supported by the business community. Such government regulation ought to be supported by the business community because it is regulation designed to support the rules of business activity itself. Practices that undermine competition either through monopoly or deceit cut away at a central tenet of business practice. From a market perspective, failure to support attempts to control and thwart such anticompetitive practices would be self-defeating.

Theory, in this regard, is supported by practice. Complaints regarding deceptive advertising often are brought to the attention of government regulators by the competitors of the alleged offender. It was competing oil companies who successfully challenged Chevron's STP advertising claims. Similarly, it was competing drug companies who complained to the Federal Trade Commission about the claims of Sterling Drug on behalf of Bayer aspirin. Sterling used a report in the *New England Journal of Medicine*, which received partial financial support from the FTC itself, as "objective" proof for the superiority of Bayer aspirin. The competing companies alleged that the ads were misleading and deceptive. That dispute went all the way to the Supreme Court, which turned down the complaints of the competing drug companies (*F.T.C.* v. *Sterling Drug*). The Bayer aspirin dispute provides a perfect illustration of business reliance on government regulation and of its use of the judiciary to settle a dispute on a rule of business practice. Such government regulation is clearly in the interest of business.

Government regulation can also serve another interest of business. In our discussion of codes of ethics in Chapter 5, it was shown how a business could be in "a prisoner's dilemma situation" with respect to some socially desirable act it wished to undertake. In a competitive system, a costly activity done on behalf of the public good (e.g., installing scrubbers to reduce air pollution) could put an individual firm at a competitive disadvantage. Its products would be more costly. In the absence of an effective code of ethics, industrywide government regulation would enable the individual firm to undertake the action that is desirable from society's point of view without incurring any competitive disadvantage. For example, by setting universal air quality control standards, all firms polluting the air would be required to install scrubbers. In this way, government regulation enables some companies to do the good they wanted to do but could not do because the competitive penalties would be too high. In such situations government regulation assists well-intentioned businesses to be the good citizens they want to be.

Yet another advantage of government regulation is that it forces indifferent or maleficent corporations to adhere to the minimum requirements of corporate social responsibility. In Chapter 2, it was argued that every corporation should adhere to at least the neoclassical definition of the function of a corporation, namely, to seek a reasonable profit consistent with the canons of justice and with respect for individual rights. Much of the growth of government regulation can be attributed to the fact that society has broadened its notion of corporate social responsibility, and hence it has increased its demand for government protection. The public demands government regulation as a check on corporate misbehavior while simultaneously expanding its list of business activities that it finds ethically inappropriate. Most recently, however, the public has pulled back from this course. Concern with declining productivity and the cost of regulation have brought about a shift in attitude. Nonetheless government protection against corporate irresponsibility (e.g., chemical dumping) is still a public goal.

In summary, the expansion of government regulation is the result of at least three factors. First, it results from the universally recognized authority of government to interpret and enforce the rules of business activity. Second, it results from requests from socially enlightened corporations that need government-imposed standards to enable them to take socially desirable actions without incurring serious competitive disadvantages. Third, it results from the demands of the general public that it be protected against a growing list of what are viewed as undesirable corporate practices.

Thomas C. Schelling has put the case for government regulation this way: You need government regulation when the firm may lack the discipline, the information, the incentives, or the moral authority to command performance or restraint on the part of everyone whose cooperation is needed.[1]

Disadvantages of Government Regulation

Despite the advantages for business of some forms of government regulation, in general government regulation is viewed on a scale from distrust to horror. There are several popular reasons why government regulation is opposed. These include

1. A recognition that government regulation would diminish the power and the prestige of corporate officials.

2. A fear that government officials would interfere with incentives and efficiency and hence reduce profit.

3. A judgment that government officials do not understand business and hence that its regulations would be unreasonable and unworkable.

4. A judgment that government officials are in no position to comment on the ethics of others.

5. A judgment that the federal government is already too powerful in a pluralistic society so that it is inappropriate to increase the power of government in this way.

6. A judgment that government regulation violates the legitimate freedom and moral rights of employers and stockholders.

Although these six items present an accurate list of the popular objections to government regulation, they provide an inadequate base for discussion. While some of the objections raise legitimate issues, for example, point 6, other objections are either too sweeping, for example, point 4, or self-serving, for example, point 1. Philosophically, what is needed is some theoretical framework to serve as the basis of criticism. My critical

---

[1] Thomas C. Schelling, "Command and Control," in *Ethical Theory and Business*, eds. Thomas L. Beauchamp and Norman E. Bowie (Englewood Cliffs, N.J.: Prentice-Hall, Inc., 1979), p. 218.

comments focus on three areas. First, I present a set of criteria that serves to evaluate both specific laws and a legal system—in other words a set of criteria that enables us to distinguish good laws from bad ones or to distinguish a good legal system from a less adequate one. These criteria will then be used to evaluate government regulations concerned with business. Our analysis of how government regulation runs afoul of the criteria for good lawmaking will give credence to the criticisms that government regulation frequently interferes with incentives and efficiency and hence reduces profit and that government regulations are frequently unreasonable and unworkable. Second, the cost–benefit approach that is the primary method used in preparing, interpreting, and enforcing government regulation will be scrutinized critically. Special attention will be directed to the notion of the public interest that is the alleged goal of decisions made on the basis of cost–benefit analysis. Third, government regulation will be criticized from the perspective of an overall political philosophy that places great value on individualism, decentralized power, reward according to merit, and property rights. It is in this context that the criticisms that government regulation would dangerously increase government power and would violate the legitimate freedom and moral rights of employers and stockholders will receive our attention.

The Criteria for Good Law

In a penetrating analysis of law (*The Morality of Law*), Lon Fuller identified eight conditions that any legal system must fulfill if it is to be considered a good legal system.[2] These eight conditions include (1) laws must be general (laws are not made to apply to one individual), (2) laws must be publicized, (3) laws cannot be made retroactively, (4) laws must be understandable, (5) the set of laws should not contain rules that are contradictory, (6) laws must be within the power of citizens to obey them, (7) laws must maintain a certain stability through time, and (8) laws as announced must be in agreement with their actual administration.

Fuller's eight conditions for a good legal system have such a ring of self-evidence about them that explanatory comments can be kept to a minimum. However, in the course of supplying some explanatory comment, the extent to which government regulation violates these eight conditions for good law will become obvious. The condition of generality is clearly related to the analyses of justice and the universalizability required by Kant's categorical imperative discussed in Chapter 3. Rules are

---

[2] Lon Fuller, *The Morality of Law*, rev. ed. (New Haven, Conn.: Yale University Press, 1964), p. 39.

not directed toward a single person but rather are to apply to a class of persons. Relevantly similar persons are to be treated similarly. What is a reason in one case must be a reason in all similar cases.

Despite this requirement of generality, much regulatory law proceeds in an opposite direction. Fuller says,

> In recent history perhaps the most notable failure to achieve general rules has been that of certain of our regulatory agencies, particularly those charged with allocative functions. . . . [T]hey were embarked on their careers in the belief that by proceeding at first case by case they would gradually gain an insight which would enable them to develop general standards of decision. In some cases this hope has been almost completely disappointed; this is notably so in the case of the Civil Aeronautics Board and the Federal Communications Commission.[3]

If general rules are essential to good regulatory law as has been argued, then the case-by-case method is inadequate. If the government takes a position regarding water pollution from one of Bethlehem Steel's plants, the president of Bethlehem Steel should be able to conclude that the government will take a similar position on similar conditions at all Bethlehem's plants. Moreover, the president of Bethlehem Steel should be able to conclude that the same position will be taken when the same situation exists at other competing steel plants. If Fuller's description is right, the state of regulatory law is such that the president of Bethlehem Steel could not conclude that a similar position would be taken and hence much regulatory law is seriously deficient.

The second condition is that the laws be publicized. This condition goes hand in hand with the conditions of generality and stability. One cannot obey the law if one does not know what the law is. Regulatory law does conform—on the whole—to this condition. The regulations do appear in federal documents such as the *Federal Register*. However, any academic researcher who has worked with government documents knows that finding a rule or regulation is often no easy task. Large corporations have legal teams to assist them in knowing what the law is. However, as government regulations grow, the small business houses suffer a distinct handicap in their capability to know the law. To the extent the regulations change rapidly over time, the publicity requirement becomes harder and harder to meet.

Third, laws should not be made retroactively, and generally they are not. The reason for this requirement is clear. Laws are designed to guide behavior. A retroactive law violates the fundamental purpose of laws since it obviously cannot guide conduct. It punishes behavior that was legal at the time it was done. Business leaders complain that government

---

[3] Ibid., p. 46.

regulators at least approach violating this condition when they threaten firms with penalties for environmental damage when there is no way for the firm to have known that some of its activities were causing environmental damage. A company should not be penalized for damage it caused to the earth's ozone layer when it produced fluorocarbons in the 1960s.

The fourth requirement of clarity is, to many business executives, the condition that government regulations most often violate. Loaded with jargon and bad grammar, these regulations often present a nightmare for highly trained corporate legal staffs and an impossible situation for small companies. A few sample selections will serve to illustrate the point:

911.341 Lime Regulation 39.

(a) During the period May 1, 1979, through June 17, 1979, no handler shall handle:

(1) Any limes of the group known as true "seeded" limes (also known as Mexican, West Indian, and Key limes and by other synonyms), grown in the production area, which do not meet the requirements of at least U.S. No. 2 Grade for Persian (Tahiti) Limes, except as to color: Provided, That true limes, grown in the production area, which fail to meet the requirements of such grade may be handled within the production area, if such limes meet all other applicable requirements of this section and the minimum juice content requirement prescribed in the U.S. Standards for Persian (Tahiti) Limes, and are handled in containers other than the containers prescribed in 911.329 for the handling of limes between the production area and any point outside thereof;[4]

212.75 Crude Oil Produced and Sold from Unitized Properties.

(b) Definitions. For purposes of this section—"Current unit cumulative deficiency" means (1) for months prior to June 1, 1979, the total number of barrels by which production and sale of crude oil from the unitized property was less than the unit base production control level subsequent to the first month (following the establishment of a unit base production control level for that unitized property) in which any crude oil produced and sold from that unit was eligible to be classified as actual new crude oil (without regard to whether the amount of actual new crude oil was exceeded by the amount of imputed new crude oil), minus the total number of barrels of domestic crude oil produced and sold in each prior month from that unitized property (following the establishment of a unit base production control level for that unitized property) which was in excess of the unit base production control level for that month, but which was not eligible to be classified as actual new crude oil because of this requirement to reduce the amount of actual new crude oil in each month by the amount of the current unit cumulative deficiency;[5]

---

[4] *Federal Register,* Vol. 44, no. 68, April 6, 1979.

[5] *Federal Register,* Vol. 44, no. 69, April 9, 1979.

Fifth, a system of laws that contains laws contradicting one another is inadequate because a situation covered by the contradictory laws requires the impossible. Fuller focuses on the federal Food, Drug, and Cosmetic Act.

> Section 704 of that act defines the conditions under which an inspector may enter a factory; one of these conditions is that he first obtain the permission of the owner. Section 331 makes it a crime for the owner of the factory to refuse "to permit entry or inspection as authorized by section 704." The Act seems, then, to say that the inspector has a right to enter the factory but that the owner has a right to keep him out by refusing permission.[6]

Actually, the instances of contradiction cited by businesspersons are not so obvious as those in the case given. Most contradictions in laws governing business practice result from two sources: (1) from contradictory rules issued by independent agencies responsible for the same area and (2) from contradictory rules issued by independent agencies on separate matters but when applied in a specific case lead to contradiction.

To illustrate just how complex the issue of the contradictory nature of law can become, consider, for example, the recent Sears suit against a number of federal agencies or officers, including the attorney general, the secretary of Labor, the chairman of the Equal Opportunity Commission (EOC), and seven other cabinet officers and federal agencies. The issue of contention is antidiscrimination statutes. Employers like Sears are not to discriminate on the basis of race, sex, age, or physical and mental handicaps. Yet the employer is required to give preference to veterans. But since veterans are overwhelmingly male, the required preference for veterans is in contradiction with the requirement that no preference be given to sex. Preferences for veterans ipso facto give preference to males. Moreover, other government programs, themselves discriminatory, make private sector nondiscriminations more difficult to achieve. For example, Sears contends that the social security system has operated in a way to keep females out of the work force and hence that government quotas to hire given percentages of women are in conflict with the laws of the social security system. It is reported that

> The Company [Sears] asked the court to grant an injunction requiring the defendants "to coordinate the employment of anti-discrimination statutes" and to issue uniform guidelines that would tell employers "how to resolve existing conflicts between affirmative-action requirements based on race and sex and those based on veterans' status, age, and physical or mental handicaps."[7]

---

[6] Fuller, The Morality of Law, p. 67.

[7] "Sears Turns the Tables," Newsweek, February 5, 1979, pp. 86–87.

Without judging either Sears' motives for the suit or its behavior with respect to nondiscrimination, the Sears request for consistency is warranted in point of logic and good law.

Sixth, laws requiring the impossible violate the fundamental purpose of law—the guidance of human conduct. This point seems so obvious that it hardly needs comment. Yet a tradition is growing in legal circles that clearly violates this principle. Strict liability holds a person or corporation liable for an act even when they are not responsible for it. Fuller points out the absurdity of allowing strict liability to expand so that it covers all activities.

> *If strict liability were to attend, not certain specified forms of activity, but all activities, the conception of a causal connection between the act and the resulting injury would be lost. A poet writes a sad poem. A rejected lover reads it and is so depressed that he commits suicide. Who "caused" the loss of his life? Was it the poet, or the lady who jilted the deceased, or perhaps the teacher who aroused his interest in poetry? A man in a drunken rage shoots his wife. Who among those concerned with this event share the responsibility for its occurrence—the killer himself, the man who lent the gun to him, the liquor dealer who provided the gin, or was it perhaps the friend who dissuaded him from securing a divorce that would have ended an unhappy alliance?[8]*

Fuller's analysis also reiterates our discussion of equal opportunity in Chapter 4. It does seem wrong to say that one's religion should not count against one but that one's lack of intelligence should. However, when you go as far as Rawls and eliminate individual responsibility for all character traits, you must give up the notion of trying to tie benefits and burdens to desert. When carried to its extreme, the very basis of law that does tie benefits and burdens to desert is undermined. So is the morality that has as its central principle "ought implies can." Presumably, some balance between Rawls and Fuller must be struck.

Hence, to conform to this requirement of good law, the government regulations of business must rest on an adequate theory that delineates a class of undesirable acts that can result from business activity and then assesses the extent to which business must be shown to be responsible for their acts before being held liable. It may well be, for example, that some activities (blasting) are so dangerous that strict liability should be invoked to discourage the activity in question. However, in many cases strict liability is not the appropriate legal category and business people are quite right in being concerned about its ever-growing application.

Another condition that seems constantly violated in the government regulation of business is Fuller's seventh requirement of constancy

---

[8] Fuller, *The Morality of Law*, p. 76.

through time. Government regulations are in a constant state of flux. One political party replaces another in the White House and the rules of the game change. Let there be a change in the leadership of a major congressional committee and the rules change again.

During the early years of the environmental crisis, companies were forced or encouraged to abandon coal because it tended to be a highly polluting fuel. Now that the energy crisis is here, companies are being encouraged or forced to return to coal to save precious oil. The expenses involved in these transitions are staggering. Something must be done to control the anarchic flux so characteristic of the government regulation of business.

Finally, there should be agreement between the law and the way it is administered. It is one thing to discover what the law is. It is quite another to have the law enforced as written. Business people argue that the federal and state regulatory bureaucracies are filled with petty individuals whose only means of gaining self-respect is by blocking the legitimate plans or aims of business. The time and effort involved in fighting these people discourages the growth of small business and encourages large businesses to provide either a psychic or monetary bribe to clear the roadblocks. There has been much talk about protecting employee rights within the firm. Devices must also be found to protect the legitimate interests of individual business from the government bureaucracy.

To balance this criticism, the reader should know that Fuller's eight conditions for good law represent an ideal for a legal system. The reader should also realize that Fuller's ideal works best for statutes; it works somewhat less well for administrative decisions. No legal system can conform completely to Fuller's ideals. Take the condition that the law must be stable through time. Change, including change in the conditions that produced the law in the first place, requires changes in the law as well. Before OPEC and the oil crisis, cleaning up the atmosphere required regulations that discouraged the burning of coal. The oil embargo changed all that. Strategic considerations required encouragement for the use of coal. This shift in policy was expensive, but, given the changes in the world situation, the shift was necessary.

Fuller would agree here. Indeed, that is why he refers to his eight conditions as constituting a morality of the ideal rather than a morality of duty. However, Fuller is right in indicating that departures from these eight conditions do have costs, including the cost of undermining the law itself. In this way Fuller fills a role with respect to the conditions for the law that Sissela Bok filled with respect to truth telling. Both have shown how even necessary departures from the ideal have important negative consequences.

Others might argue that regulatory law is something of a misnomer.

Regulatory "law" has less in common with law than it does with judicial decisions or executive decisions. What constitutes the disanalogy, Fuller's critics believe, is that judicial decisions or executive decisions are geared to specific situations and hence have less of the characteristic of generality than do statutes. Fuller might concede much of this point yet insist, correctly I believe, that his eight conditions still serve as an ideal for judicial and executive decisions as well. After all, Supreme Court *decisions* are viewed by everyone as establishing precedents. Perhaps the rule for the pricing of gas at the pumps need not be clear to everyone, but it should at least be clear to the oil companies, shouldn't it?

With these cautions in mind, Fuller's eight conditions for good law are fundamentally sound. Even when Fuller's eight conditions are recognized as an ideal, the fact that so much government regulatory policy stands in violation of them points out a serious inadequacy in the use of government regulation for achieving ethical corporate behavior. After all, government through its judicial system and through some regulation is, as we have seen, a requirement for a stable business environment. Both the law and business are rule-governed activities. When the rules that apply to business or that sustain and protect business violate the conditions for good law, business is harmed. Laws that are not stable do adversely affect incentives and efficiency. Laws that are not clear or that require the impossible, or that apply retroactively, or that are contradictory are unreasonable and unworkable. Both the business community and the public at large have every right to insist that the laws regulating business should conform to the criteria for good law.

The Public Good and Cost–Benefit Analysis

A broad-based justification for government regulation is an appeal to the public good. Politicians argue that some new government regulation is needed to protect the American public from the greed of some special interest group. But what is the public interest?

The first problem is a conceptual one. I usually know what my interests are. They are individual and specific to me. The same is true of my responsibilities. But what of the interests and responsibilities of a corporation, a government, a public? These entities are collective entities, and when we speak of them in this context we are speaking of collective interests and collective responsibilities. But do such concepts as collective responsibility and the public good make any sense?

Let us begin with the notion of corporate responsibility. Does it make any sense to speak of the responsibility of a corporation independently of the responsibility of the individuals that make it up? Some writers like Peter French have argued that such ascriptions of corporate responsibility make perfect sense. The key in an account like French's is the rules (a charter and bylaws, for example) that indicate what counts as the purpose of the corporation and how an activity of some individuals within the corporation can be designated officially as an action of the corporation. An order by a chief executive can *only* be a matter of company policy if that order is in conformity to the rules. Similarly, a decision made in conformity with the rules is a decision of the corporation, even if *no member* of the corporation agrees with the decision in all respects. Often, it is sufficient that a majority of the officers vote in favor of the policy. A corporation has no difficulty in understanding the notion of collective responsibility when it issues its annual report. Similarly, it should have no difficulty in taking collective responsibility for at least some actions that deserve blame or praise. As French says,

> *It is sobering to keep in mind that the Gulf Oil Company certainly knows what "You are held responsible for payment in full of the amount recorded on your statement" means. [Similarly it can understand what] "The Gulf Oil Corporation should be held responsible for destroying the ecological balance of the bay" means.*[9]

But now let us try to apply French's analysis to the public good as the public interest. What is government in the public interest?

By extending French's analysis, we could say that any action of government is government in the public interest so long as that action is in accordance with the purpose or function of government (is constitutional) and is taken in accordance with the rules. On such an interpretation, government in the public interest is primarily a procedural notion. The substantive element is provided by the substantive elements in the Constitution itself. Is such a notion sufficient?

The notion of procedural justice has already been frequently employed in this book. As you recall, we must distinguish between just procedures and just results. In a gambling situation, the emphasis is on just procedures. So long as the dice are not fixed, the results are just—even if the richest persons are winners. However, the practices of most institutions are not like gambling. We are concerned with both just procedures and just results.

A popular argument on behalf of the procedures of American democracy is known as interest group liberalism. In this view, society is composed of a number of competing interest groups with overlapping individual membership. Within a framework of rules, these various groups struggle with one another to determine how a given policy will be deter-

---

[9] Peter French, "Corporate Moral Agency," Thomas L. Beauchamp and Norman E. Bowie, p. 186.

mined. On the first level, it might be said that the public good is simply identical with the decision made as a result of the rule-governed struggle of competing interest groups. However, such a conclusion would surely be false unless several important assumptions are made.

We must assume that all individuals are members of interest groups, that emerging or less powerful interest groups are not discriminated against, and that all interest groups have a fair number of wins. Interest groups, like individuals, must achieve something approximating equality of results; equal opportunity is not sufficient. Some comment on this last contention is in order.

In our political system, the benefits of citizenship are guaranteed to all. One need not win out in a competitive struggle for those benefits the way one needs to win out in a competitive struggle for a higher salary. Each citizen has a right to at least a minimum amount of the benefits of citizenship. The same argument applies to organizations of citizens to whom I have referred as interest groups. Having identified the assumptions that must hold if one is to claim that the public good is simply identical with the results of the struggle among competing interest groups, I think it is obvious that the assumptions may not hold, and hence it is doubtful if the public good is identical with the results of the struggle.

A further complication is added when you consider the intensity that an individual or group has for or against a certain policy. Suppose that most people are quite indifferent (only slightly in favor) toward some proposed action but that a small minority is intensely opposed. Should the intensity of the minority be counted in (weighted), or should everyone's vote count for one and only one?

To begin addressing that issue is to immediately raise another important issue. Whether or not intensity should count depends in part on the issue being discussed. If a proposed action violates the rights of the minority, the intensity of the opposition demands attention. Note, however, that it is not the intensity of the negative feelings of the minority that deserves recognition but, rather, the fact that their rights are being violated. Intensity of feelings does not merit any special consideration. After all, the moral damage created when individual rights are ignored is just as serious when the victims say nothing as it is when the victims vehemently protest. What is needed in any discussion of the public interest is some framework for deciding which interests the public has are the legitimate concern of government. Not all the interests that the individual members of the public have are the appropriate concern of government. These individual interests should be excluded from any notion of what constitutes the public interest.

On the other hand, isn't it reasonable to believe that there are some interests that, although not the interest of any particular interest group, are, nonetheless, a part of the public interest.

> *America is growing uglier, more dangerous, and less pleasant to live in, as its*
> *citizens grow richer. The reason is that natural beauty, public order, the*
> *cultivation of the arts, are not the special interest of any identifiable social*
> *group.*[10]

In summary, it seems as if the goal of defining what "public interest" refers to has at least partially eluded us. We cannot assume that the public interest will evolve by some invisible hand from the struggle among competing interest groups. Neither can we assume that every interest group represents an interest that is a legitimate concern of government. Nor can we assume that every interest that is a legitimate concern of government is represented by an interest group. An adequate theory of what does count as the public interest lies beyond the scope of a book in business ethics.

Let us now turn to the technique of cost–benefit analysis, which is used primarily as the measuring rod for determining the public interest. Indeed, cost–benefit analysis is commonly employed by both business and government. For example, the basis for many corporate social audits as well as other measures of corporate performance is cost–benefit analysis.

The idea behind cost–benefit procedures is that one can *measure numerically* costs and benefits yet, at the same time, identify uncertainties and possible trade-offs, to present policy makers or businesspersons with specific, relevant information on the basis of which a decision can be reached. Although such analysis usually proceeds by measuring different quantitative units (e.g., the number of worker accidents, statistical deaths, dollars expended, and number of workers fired), cost–benefit analysis by its very methodology attempts in the end to convert and express these seemingly incommensurable units of measurement into a common one, usually a monetary unit. It is this ultimate reduction that gives the method its power, because judgments about trade-offs can be made on the basis of perfectly comparable quantities. For example, it has been argued that among its other uses it can be employed to make financially explicit such trade-offs (reached in government policy decisions) as those between environmental quality and factory productivity and those between the quality of gasoline and the quality of the health of those who produce it.

Cost–benefit analysis has been widely criticized as a technique, especially when suggested for public policy purposes. First, the method has proved difficult to implement. Economists have been largely concerned to spell out how such analyses can be carried out in *theory* rather than to provide practical and already quantified examples. The fact that many important variables are difficult to ascertain and quantify reliably—so difficult that we may never be very confident about the ending

---

[10] Robert Paul Wolff, *The Poverty of Liberalism* (Boston: Beacon Press, 1969), p. 159.

net sum—is a major reason why it has seemed to many a nonviable technique. This conclusion has been particularly drawn in the case of evaluating projects that would improve the quality of life, as opposed to considerations merely about the purchase of capital goods. The use of cost–benefit analysis may skew policy making in an unfortunate direction. The more one is committed to precise quantitative results, the more one must focus on the short term, since that is the time frame that is the most predictable and calculable. However, many social problems need long-range analysis as well. Failure to provide it is exceedingly dangerous as the current energy crisis illustrates. We simply have not planned for the depletion of fossil fuels; nor have we planned for the ultimate removal of nuclear wastes. Of course, *once* we start planning, quantitative methods will be very helpful. However, the quantitative cost–benefit method by itself does not get the right questions asked. One must go beyond the cost–benefit analysis approach if one is to use that approach to problem solving effectively.

A second and important objection to cost–analysis that has been put forward by some writers is that we may not want it for *moral* reasons, and most especially for reasons of distributive justice. It may be that some cost–benefit analyses will tell us that a particular device would be highly beneficial as compared with its costs, and yet provision of this benefit might function in an economy to deny more basic services to the poor. Perhaps instead, as a matter of justice, the poor ought to be subsidized, either in terms of services or financial awards, even if the subsidy would not be justified on strict cost–benefit grounds. When this problem is coupled with the generally acknowledged fact that the language of "costs" and "benefits" itself harbors implicit value judgments about positive and negative consequences, it looks as if some fundamental moral thinking must be done not only about whether to accept a particular cost–benefit model as decisive, but also about the acceptability of the *notions* of costs and benefits. In other words, the terms "cost" and "benefit" are not simple factual terms like "six feet tall" or "weighs a hundred pounds." Every one would agree that if a validated scale shows that these twelve oranges weigh one pound, the oranges do weigh one pound. We cannot assume that everyone will agree that more efficient automobile travel or a larger number of television stations are benefits. And many people will certainly not agree that sacrificing an important interest of an individual for the so-called public good is always morally appropriate.

Further Limitations of Government Regulation

The failure of much regulatory law to meet Fuller's eight conditions for law and the shortsightedness of many practitioners of cost–benefit analysis are in principle correctable. We can improve our theory of the public interest, and we can become more sophisticated in our use of cost–benefit analysis. However, even if such improvements could be effected, government regulation is not completely adequate.

In his excellent book, *Where the Law Ends*, Christopher Stone shows that the nature of law itself prevents it from being a sufficient condition for achieving corporate responsibility. Most businesspersons have already moved beyond the point at which they believe the law is the final word in setting standards of corporate ethics. The view "If it's legal, it's O.K." is not the prevailing notion in most corporations.

Nonetheless, the first response of the public, whenever it is unhappy, is to argue for the passage of new laws. If Stone's analysis is correct, this constant attempt to regulate corporate conduct through law is doomed to failure. First, there is the time lag problem. Laws are passed only after the damage has been done, and often the damage is severe. What is needed is some way of preventing the damage in the first place. We cannot look to the law for that.

Second, there are limitations connected with the making of law. Stone observes that corporations play a very large role in formulating the law that governs them. Stone is *not* saying that corporations engage in bribery or intimidation to attain such influence; rather, Stone's point is that there is a natural corporate influence on the lawmaking process. After all, who has the expertise to know what regulations are reasonable? Is it not the corporations themselves? This expertise is usually a function of being in possession of relevant data that others cannot obtain—or at least cannot obtain without unwarranted difficulty. As Stone says,

> The companies most closely associated with the problems may not know the answers either, but they certainly have the more ready access to the most probative information. It is their doctors who treat the employees' injuries; it is their chemists who live with and test the new compounds; it is their health records that gather absentee data.[11]

If the commonly held view that regulatory boards have as their members representatives of the industry being regulated is correct, such a phenomenon has a readily understandable explanation.

But corporate influence over the laws that regulate them is not the only inherent difficulty that stands in the way of implementing the law. Most decisions of public policy are inordinately complex. Consider nuclear power in the era of the energy crisis. It is clear that the waste disposal problem has never been addressed satisfactorily and that the accident at the Three Mile Island facility near Harrisburg, Pennsylvania raises serious questions about plant safety. Nonetheless, electrical energy is heavily dependent on oil, coal is a serious air pollutant, and the

---

[11] C. D. Stone, *Where the Law Ends* (New York: Harper & Row, Publishers, 1975), p. 96.

widespread use of solar power is not immediately technically or economically feasible. Given this dismal range of alternatives, how stringent should the regulation of nuclear power plants be? There simply is no consensus on the value issues in such a decision. As a society, we cannot agree on how the various issues are to be weighted. Without a majority consensus on the value issues, regulations that will be stable and enforceable are extremely hard to provide.

Another difficulty concerns the assignment of responsibility—of tracing the line of causal connections so that we can determine who has been injured and who has perpetuated the injury. The adversary model of law presupposes the ability of a judge or jury to make that kind of determination. But most issues of corporate responsibility do not easily fit into that model. As Stone says,

> The food we will eat tonight (grown, handled, packaged, distributed by various corporations) may contain chemicals that are killing us, or at least reducing our life expectancy, considerably. But (a) we cannot know with certainty the fact that we are being injured by any particular product; (b) it is difficult determining who might be injuring us—that is, even if we know that our bodies are suffering a build-up of mercury, we are faced with an awesome task of pinning responsibility on any particular source of mercury; (c) we would have a difficult time proving the extent of our injuries . . .[12]

What such an example shows is that in many cases we cannot have much confidence in our ability to trace out the causal connections. Causal analysis works best in those cases where it is relatively easy to talk of the cause of some specific event. As you move away from that paradigm, causal analysis becomes less effective.

Third, there are problems with vagueness. Some vagueness problems are inherent in language itself. The issues associated with those problems have been discussed on pages 96–97. However, when society attempts to draft laws to apply in situations in which there is no consensus on what ought to be done and in which it is difficult to determine causes and effects, the vagueness problem is much more serious. Harried lawmakers are forced to use broad, general terminology. Since the law cannot be directed to a specific cause and a specific effect, useless generality is to be expected. Besides, the legislator must satisfy the demands of those who "want something done" yet at the same time draft a law that could receive a majority vote. Platitudinous generalities are ideal in such a situation.

However, the legislative compromise soon becomes the administrators' nightmare. These vague laws must be fleshed out with

---

[12] Ibid., p. 104.

regulations. But regulations that evolve from the idiosyncratic views of individual bureaucrats rather than from a background of legislative intent are often cumbersome, inconsistent, and trivial. Any corporation that tries to abide by such regulations feels harassed. Any corporation cited as being in violation of the regulations feels unjustifiably singled out for punishment. As a result, the entire climate becomes poisoned and the broader and more important moral questions are lost in the daily battles between the government and the corporation.

Fourth and last, the law is often a prohibitively expensive means for regulating corporate behavior. It works reasonably well when it seeks to establish minimum standards for corporate conduct. It works much less well when it addresses ideals. High moral standards that exceed industry norms are like high product quality standards that exceed industry norms. They result from the decisions of high-minded persons; they do not come about from legislation. Any attempt to legislate ideals will result in high costs in implementation and enforcement. Laws have costly side effects. Consider the issue of drug safety laws. The stricter the controls, the greater the public's protections against injury from harmful drugs. But the stricter the controls, the longer the time lag between the discovery of a drug and its availability to the general public. In the time lag, persons suffer and often die because that drug is not available. A possible example of inappropriate legislation is the so-called Delaney clause to the 1958 Food Additives amendment to the federal Food, Drug, and Cosmetic Act. That clause bans any food or drug that has been shown to cause cancer in laboratory animals. Yet artificial sweeteners are essential to the fight against diabetes and obesity. In a society where artificial sweeteners are banned, the deaths from the effects of obesity are likely to exceed the deaths from cancer. Is not the goal of zero cancer deaths an unreasonable ideal? The law must set minimum standards, but it is not an effective vehicle for achieving ideals.

There are other costs, not mentioned by Stone, associated with government regulation. Some have argued that there is a substantial bias on the part of regulatory personnel to keep finding things wrong so that they would have something to regulate. After all, they are rewarded and promoted for doing something for their pay. Policemen are expected to make a certain number of arrests. IRS agents are supposed to uncover a certain amount of income tax fraud. Anecdotes like the following abound. A company expects a visit from OSHA officials. Although the company has been most scrupulous in following OSHA rules, it realizes the OSHA officials cannot leave the plant empty-handed (without citing some violations). Hence, company officials create a few easily fixable minor violations so that the OSHA officials have something to cite. After the OSHA officials leave, the violations are removed. My point here is that the career interests of the regulators create pressures for over regulation.

On the basis of these arguments the case is made that there are features of law that make it an inappropriate vehicle as an exclusive instrument of state policy for achieving the good society.

Government Regulation and the Clash of Values

Government regulation is sometimes necessary and often desirable. Yet government regulation is frequently limited and occasionally dangerous. This dual nature of government regulation can be illustrated through a discussion of the effects of increasing government regulation on traditional American values. As our basic values have shifted, government regulation has seemed an ideal vehicle to protect and enrich these newly emerging values. However, the growth of government regulation has undercut and diminished other traditional values—values that many Americans agree should be supplemented by other values but values that nearly all Americans agree should not be destroyed. To what extent does government regulation interfere with certain values long accepted by American society? This debate is often framed along the following lines: values such as individualism, reward according to merit, well-entrenched property rights, equal opportunity, and individual autonomy (particularly in economic matters) are taken as *desirata*. It is then argued that the operation of the marketplace is supportive of these values, while the operation of government bureaucracies is inimical to them. Hence, any increase in government regulation threatens basic values.[13]

Let us construct an anecdote that shows how many Americans believe the traditional value system works within the free market context. Mr. and Mrs. Chovosky and their two children immigrate to the United States from a totalitarian Eastern European country. Mr. Chovosky finds employment as an unskilled assembly-line worker and part-time employment on the weekends as a janitor. The Chovosky family finds an apartment in a suitable ethnic neighborhood and sends their children to the neighborhood schools. Through hard work, Mr. Chovosky rises to a pressman's position and is eventually able to buy a small home. Mr. Chovosky's two sons become high school football stars as well as competent students. Both are offered college scholarships. After attending college, one becomes a successful doctor, the other a successful attorney. They both marry "well"—daughters of established American families. Mr. Chovosky dies at age seventy-two, secure in the knowledge that his children are now full participants in the American dream.

Most Americans would see this anecdote as a fairly accurate ac-

---

[13] For a well-argued recent statement of this position, see Paul H. Weaver, "Regulations, Social Policy, and Class Conflict," *The Public Interest*, Vol 50 (Winter 1978), 45–63.

count of what the American dream is all about. Through *individual hard work,* one climbs the ladder of social and economic success (*is rewarded according to his or her merit*). To ensure the fairness, all citizens are guaranteed equal opportunity in the sense they are (1) free to rise from one social class to another, (2) not to be discriminated against on the basis of race, religion, or national origin, and (3) entitled to a free public education. What is needed for success is a combination of hard work and ability. One is entitled to the economic and social rewards obtained.

The free competitive market, it is argued, is the most effective way of organizing economic institutions to support these values. Since the market is profit oriented, the only personal characteristics that really count are characteristics related to efficient production, specifically ability and hard work. Race, religion, class origin, and ethnic background do not matter. Moreover, the market responds to, rather than dictates, consumer choice. In a market economy, the consumer is sovereign. Hence, the market respects individual freedom and autonomy, is supportive of equal opportunity, and produces efficiently a cornucopia of material goods and services. Many would agree that the free market economy is the most likely way to make the Chovosky story a reality.

Experience reminds us, however, that in the competitive struggle for the good life, there are many losers as well. As our attention has turned to the losers, both ideology and our view of the basically unregulated free market have undergone a significant shift. This ideological shift has received some attention in our discussion of equal opportunity in Chapter 4. A more extensive discussion of the fall of the traditional ideology has been provided by George Cabot Lodge in an article "Managerial Implications of Ideological Change."[14]

One of the strongest challenges was launched against the notion of individualism. An early phase of the attack focused on the Latin phrase *caveat emptor* (let the buyer beware). *Caveat emptor* had long been accepted as one of the costs of consumer sovereignty and individual freedom. The consumers were free to spend their money as they saw fit. However, they had to accept the consequences if they spent it foolishly.

Caveat emptor may not have been an unreasonable view to take in an economy where (1) the buyer and seller knew each other, (2) the commodities that were exchanged were familiar, simple, and designed to meet basic needs, and (3) the commodities had been produced by the seller. The American economy, however, has little relation to the economy just described. Buyers and sellers seldom know each other; the commodities exchanged are "new and improved," complex and mass produced to meet

---

[14] George Cabot Lodge, "Managerial Implications of Ideological Change," in *The Ethics of Corporate Conduct,* ed. Clarence Walton (Englewood Cliffs, N.J.: Prentice-Hall, Inc., 1977), pp. 79–105.

demands for leisure, status, and/or pleasure. The average consumer simply lacks the information for the attitude of *caveat emptor* to make any sense. In an efficient economy of mass-produced goods characterized by a high technology, the consumer must be protected if he or she is to be persuaded to purchase the goods in such an economy. The collapse of *caveat emptor* helped to create new demands for government regulation. Various state insurance commissions, state licensing agencies as well as the Federal Trade Commission, and the Securities and Exchange Commission serve as paradigm cases of regulatory agencies designed to protect the public. After the bank failures of the Great Depression, the Federal Deposit Insurance Corporation was set up to protect the savings of the average American. To demand an end to *caveat emptor* is to increase pressures for government regulation.

As the influence of the social sciences grew, the notion that "to each according to his merit" is an appropriate principle of distributive justice was called into question. As scholars examined the family, peer groups, ethnic enclaves, and other social units, the individual did not appear to be the appropriate place to begin in an analysis of social phenomena. Individuals did not enter the competitive market free of the influences of the groups to which they belong. Work habits, attitudes, and abilities were in part the result of the luck of the genes and in part the luck of family circumstances. The hard-working white male who "made it," but who was the son of a wealthy, highly motivated couple who had spared no expense in giving their son everything they could to give him a good start in life, cannot say about persons in less fortunate circumstances, "if they had only worked as hard as I did, they could have done just as well." The notion of "his merit" became amorphous. Often, what is one's "merit" is in part the "merit" of others. To concede that one's merit is to a considerable extent determined by both the action of others and by social institutions is to undercut that notion of individual responsibility upon which "to each according to his merit" is based. It is also to undercut the notion that the proper unit for measuring the effects of policy is the individual. Consequently, such notions as "the good of the company" and "the good of society" joined "individual good" as appropriate considerations in discussions of distributive justice.

However, to allow collective good, especially society's good, to count is to encourage some institution to speak on behalf of the collective entity. The appropriate social unit to discuss society's good is government. Government soon had an interest in and an authority to enact regulations that affect the distribution of goods and services. Historical circumstances mirror the analysis.

After recognizing the difficulties in determining genuine merit, it is natural to turn to an emphasis on equality of results rather than on equal opportunity. Under the traditional view of equal opportunity, the chief concern was on the fairness of the race itself, not on the number of winners. However, if "being a loser" was not totally or even basically the fault of the individual, the "losers" in society demanded not only a fair race but some of the rewards. The Great Depression produced few winners and large numbers of losers. The causal connection between merit and success was henceforth under a great cloud of suspicion. It then became the function of government to redistribute some of the prizes from the "winners" to the "losers." Progressive taxation, the minimum wage, and various welfare programs all reflect society's growing concern for greater equality of results. Indeed, the emphasis on equality of results has reached a point of alarming some social commentators. They fear that too many Americans ignore the causal connection between production and distribution; they forget that there are no prizes if prizes are not produced. One may debate how responsible the most productive citizens are for those characteristics that make them high producers. Whatever the outcome of that debate, however, it is the most productive that make "prizes" possible, and if we take too much from them, there will be fewer prizes for everyone. Whether or not such commentators are justified in their current concern, it is clear that members of society not only insist on a fair race, but they insist on obtaining some of the prizes. Their demands can only be achieved through the action of government.

However, the results of the 1980 Presidential and Congressional elections seem to show that society has become concerned with productivity as well. There must be tradeoffs between encouraging production and demands for equality of results. To grant government the authority to redistribute income is to interfere with a person's right to property. In the traditional value system, a person's income is a form of personal property. To deprive one of part of one's income through taxation is to deprive one of one's property just as if government officials took one of two cars or two radios and gave them to someone else. Does not a person have a right to his or her personal property including his or her income?

The answer, of course, is yes and no. A person is morally obligated to pay his or her fair share of the cost of public goods (e.g., national defense, public education, and police protection) regardless of whether he or she wants to or not. The amount of natural resources devoted to public goods is determined in the political arena. It is a collective decision implemented by government rather than an individual decision implemented through the market. A person's property rights are legitimately circumscribed by that political decision and that circumspection has been accepted. However, as the interdependence of people has been recognized, more and more goods have been declared "public." A private airfield adversely affects the property values of individuals located near the airport. Air and water pollution, the quality of schools, and the existence of adequate public parks affect the property of individuals. Most private property, until recently, had little effect on the life-styles of others. A person's cabin, mules, and apple tree were his. The holding of such property seldom harmed or deprived another. However, a person's car, television, and CB radio can harm another, and one's possession of these commodities may deprive another of more basic goods. Since much of our ownership of private property does affect others for good or ill, government is seen as the proper means for resolving disputes among property owners. Since the production of society's goods and services is viewed as a collective effort—at least in part—there will be increased demands that redistribution from the wealthy to the less fortunate is a morally appropriate task of government. For both reasons, individual private property rights will be further circumscribed.

A thorough examination of these issues would take us beyond business ethics to the broadest issues in social and political philosophy. The careful reader will note a general theme underlying the specific discussions. The market economy and business activity that constitutes it has traditionally emphasized individual effort and individual responsibility. This point can be exhibited in the following quotation by Tibor Machan and Alan Reynolds:

> An alternative individualist morality, more in keeping with America's cultural and political tradition, does not lend automatic support to government regulation. Indeed, in such areas as treatment of the accused, the legal status of those deemed to be mentally disturbed, and intrusion by governments into people's private affairs, we make implicit use of moral notions that would appear to be equally applicable to deregulatory efforts.
>
> Consider the idea of unjust discrimination. Imposing burdens upon members of a group on grounds that some of those members have acted improperly is generally considered unjust, especially when the practice is made public policy. The basis for this judgment is an individualist morality—the idea that individuals should be treated as individuals rather than as members of a group. Yet regulatory practices discriminate against entire groups of professionals, such as business managers or accountants, on grounds that only some of them have abused their unregulated professional opportunities.[15]

As these notions of individual effort and responsibility are subjected to criticism and come to play a less important role in a society's hierarchy of values, the responsibilities of government, which is a collective enterprise, are likely to increase.

However, the traditional values surrounding the notions of individual effort and responsibility do have a legitimate place in the good society. To provide a philosophical argument for the fundamental place that respect for individual persons holds in our society is beyond the scope of this book. The fact that all our social institutions, including

---

[15] *The New York Times,* July 8, 1978, p. 19.

business, presuppose the value of respect for individual autonomy will serve as sufficient argument. As government regulation is increased to protect the individual, the costs to traditional values have to be taken into account.

Conclusion

This completes our discussion of government regulation. In the early chapters, I have built a case for the centrality of ethics in the business life and I have tried to develop some of the central themes in the discussion and practice of business ethics. Moreover, I have discussed self-regulation and government regulation as basic techniques for enabling business practice to reflect these ethical ideals. Both have strengths and weaknesses, and hence they must be used together. In the concluding chapter, I confront the genuine dilemmas that occur when the practice of morality involves personal or corporate costs.

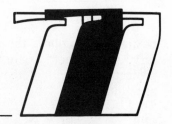

Whistle Blowing and Other Why Be Moral Questions

In Chapter 3, it was argued that business practice presupposes a commitment on the part of business to a certain morality, specifically a commitment to a minimum standard of justice and to the acknowledgment of and respect for individual human rights. It was further argued that failure to honor this commitment would result in a self-defeating act, since the universalization of the act would undermine the practice of business itself. Such arguments, however, do not settle the matter. First, nothing has been said about the dilemmas faced by employees who are ordered by superiors to commit illegal or immoral acts. Second, nothing has been said to persuade an individual company to be moral when the company can get away with it. Such a company might well acknowledge that the immoral act it commits would, *if* universalized, undermine business practice itself. However, the company goes on to argue that, since the act will *not in fact* be universalized, there is no reason why they should not do it. The final chapter in this book considers these two questions in turn.

Ethical Dilemmas for the Individual

Recently, I was a guest faculty member for a class on personnel management at a community college in a prosperous medium-sized Eastern city. I asked the students, most of whom worked, how many of them had been asked by their employer or supervisor to do something they considered illegal or immoral. Over 50 percent of the students in the class raised their hands. I then asked if some of the students would volunteer to describe the situations they faced. After some initial hesitation, I received a startling array of examples.

The Office Call Girl

One woman indicated that she had been assigned the task of "entertaining" business executives who visited her employers. Should she accept the assignment?

The Dirty Needle

A new nurse in a local hospital discovered that syringes for injections were being transmitted through the hospital's tube system without their protective covers. In other words, the points of the syringes were exposed and subject to contamination. Such a practice posed grave risks to patients. The new employee was told to be quiet and not to be a troublemaker. What should she do?

The Forged Document

A young man had his first "real" job as an employee in a local bank. Some problems arose concerning one of the accounts and the man's supervisor asked him to forge a signature. What should he do?

The Disappearing Apartments

Another woman managed a group of apartment buildings on behalf of a foreign owner. He asked her to keep two sets of books. The income reported to the foreign government would reflect receipts from only a portion of the apartment buildings. What should she do?

It seems fairly clear that, in each of the cases, the employee was asked to do something that was immoral and/or illegal. Yet, in each case, if the employee refused to do as he or she were told, serious repercussions, including the likely loss of the job, would follow. In each of the cases, the employee refused to cooperate. The woman who refused to serve as office call girl was lucky. Her supervisor, who was mishandling office funds, was fired before he could fire her. Apparently, other women who had refused were not so lucky. The foreign owner of the apartment complexes accepted his employee's explanation that it is simply impossible to keep two sets of books. In the other three cases, the employees resigned rather than perform the actions requested of them. The bank employee now has a damaging letter in his file.

Of course, I had no opportunity to investigate these cases. I do not know the complete circumstances nor do I know whether the statements I received are accurate. Investigation has been done on other cases, however. Immoral or illegal demands of employees by employers occur both in government and in business. All immoral or illegal demands of employees by employers create rather serious dilemmas for the individual. As we saw in Chapter 1, the law of agency *permits* employees to disobey immoral or illegal demands. However, as we also saw, the employee is not protected if the employer fires him or her. What should the employee do? Before answering that question, let us consider a special individual case.

Recently, another type of ethical dilemma has received considerable public attention. An employee is often in a position to know about the illegal or immoral actions of a supervisor or employer whether or not he or she is asked to participate in the act. Should an employee who is asked to participate in an illegal or immoral or who witnesses the illegal or immoral action of a supervisor or employer inform the public? Whenever these questions are answered in the affirmative and the public is informed, we have cases of whistle blowing. On a first account, whistle blowing is the act by an employee of informing the public on the immoral or illegal behavior of an employer or supervisor.

One of the better known cases in which whistle blowers have lost their jobs is the BART case. BART is the acronym for the Bay Area Rapid Transit system, a modern rail transit system in the San Francisco area. During the construction of the mass transit line, three engineers became deeply concerned with the safety of certain features of the system. Holger Hjortsvang reported, to no avail, his concerns about the Automatic Train Control System that was being built by the Westinghouse Corporation. Just a few months later, another engineer, Robert Bruder, became concerned about Westinghouse's lack of tests on certain equipment. Still later, Max Blankenzee, a senior programmer, joined Mr. Hjortsvang in his reservations. Having received no response from various memoranda, the three engineers met with a member of the BART board of directors. Following the meeting, confidential memos shared with board member Helex appeared in the *Contra Costa Times,* and the report of a private consultant in support of the three engineers was ridiculed after being presented to the full board. Three days later all three engineers were fired. The engineers sued and each won $25,000 in an out-of-court settlement. It took from eight to fifteen months for the three engineers to find satisfactory jobs elsewhere. In addition to the economic stress, the psychological stress was relatively severe on all of them.

Despite the apparent injustice that results when whistle blowers protect the public interest at great personal cost, many businesspersons have little sympathy for them. According to these businesspersons, whistle blowers have violated one of the chief duties of an employee—the duty to be loyal to one's employer. This attitude is perhaps best captured in remarks by James M. Roche, former president of General Motors.

> *Some critics are now busy eroding another support of free enterprise—the loyalty of a management team, with its unifying values of cooperative work. Some of the enemies of business now encourage an employee to be disloyal to the enterprise. They want to create suspicion and disharmony, and pry into the proprietary interests of the business. However this is labelled—industrial espionage, whistle blowing, or professional responsibility—it is another tactic for spreading disunity and creating conflict.*[1]

However, the obligation of loyalty as an overriding obligation has already been sufficiently criticized in Chapters 1 and 3. One has a duty to be loyal only if the object of loyalty is one that is morally appropriate.

One cannot assume, however, that the claims of all whistle blowers are obviously true and that the denials of all employers are obviously false. Some whistle blowers may be trying to seize more power within the company. BART made just such a charge against Hjortsvang. Other persons try to create a whistle blowing case for the purpose of covering up genuine personal inadequacies—inadequacies that represent the real reason for their being disciplined or dismissed. What is needed is a careful definition of whistle blowing and a set of conditions that indicates what considerations should be taken into account to justify acts of whistle blowing.

A discussion of whistle blowing in the 1980s is parallel to the discussions of civil disobedience in the 1960s. Just as the civil disobedients of that time appealed to a higher morality to justify overriding the *prima facie* duty to obey the laws of the state, today's whistle blowers appeal to a higher morality to override the *prima facie* duty to be loyal to one's company or firm. In this analogy, whistle blowing is a form of moral protest or dissent. It also represents a classic case of a conflict of interest as that phrase was defined in Chapter 5. The employer must decide whether to honor his or her duty to his or her employer or to honor his or her duty to

---

[1] James M. Roche, "The Competitive System, to Work, to Preserve, and to Protect," *Vital Speeches of the Day* (May 1971), 445.

a higher morality. However, by appealing to the term "higher," we already have the answer to the question, "What is the moral thing to do in such conflicts?" One ought, of course, to obey the higher moral duty.

The material from Chapters 2 and 3 will serve us well in defining a whistle blower.

> *A whistle blower is an employee or officer of any institution, profit or non-profit, private or public, who believes either that he/she has been ordered to perform some act or he/she has obtained knowledge that the institution is engaged in activities which a) are believed to cause unnecessary harm to third parties, b) are in violation of human rights or c) run counter to the defined purpose of the institution and who inform the public of this fact.*[2]

With respect to business corporations, the discerning reader will note that the whistle blower in business reports activities that violate either the basic moral presuppositions on which the business enterprise rests or that violate the purpose of corporate enterprise. The theoretical structure presented in earlier chapters provides the conceptual apparatus for distinguishing whistle blowing from tattling on the one hand and sabotage on the other.

What can be said on behalf of this definition? First, it limits the class of moral infractions that an employee should make public. A person who makes a point of informing on every indiscretion is a nuisance and is more appropriately an object of scorn rather than an object of praise. Who wants to know every time someone utters an unkind word about one's supervisor or uses a piece of office stationery for a personal letter. Parents encourage their children not to tattle. Persons in the business world should not be tattletales either. Whistle blowing is reserved conceptually only for those serious moral faults spelled out in the definition. Of course, persons who commit these relatively minor moral faults ought not to do them. An injunction against tattling does not make the actions of the perpetrators blameless. Rather, the injunction against tattling is based on the view that it is inappropriate for everyone to have as his or her responsibility for informing the authorities of the minor moral faults of everyone else. Given the rancor and ill will that are caused when people do tattle, there are good utilitarian arguments against tattling. In addition, the definition limits the scope of one's response to immoral behavior. A whistle blower's responsibility is limited to informing the public. The responsibility does not extend to taking any retaliatory action against the employer or firm. The concept of "whistle blower" must be kept distinct from the concept of "saboteur."

---

[2] Both this definition and the subsequent discussion have been strongly influenced by a yet unpublished paper of Sissela Bok's entitled "Whistle Blowing and Professional Responsibilities."

To define the whistle blower is not thereby to justify all acts of whistle blowing. The definition of something is one thing; its justification is another. The following list of conditions, when met, provide evidence that an act of whistle blowing is justified. An act of whistle blowing is justified if

1. It is done from the appropriate moral motive, namely, as provided in the definition of whistle blowing.
2. The whistle blower, except in special circumstances, has exhausted all internal channels for dissent before informing the public.
3. The whistle blower has made certain that his or her belief that inappropriate actions are ordered or have occurred is based on evidence that would persuade a reasonable person.
4. The whistle blower has acted after a careful analysis of the danger: (a) how serious is the moral violation, (b) how immediate is the moral violation, (c) is the moral violation one that can be specified?
5. The whistle blower's action is commensurate with one's responsibility for avoiding and/or exposing moral violations.
6. It has some chance of success.

This list of justifying conditions deserves some comment. The question of motive is extremely important. Since whistle blowing does violate a *prima facie* duty of loyalty to one's employer, whistle blowing must be based on moral grounds if it is to be justified. The moral aim of whistle blowing is deemed so central that it is made part of the definition, namely, whistle blowing aims at exposing unnecessary harm, violation of human rights, or conduct counter to the defined purpose of the corporation. However, the moral dimensions of whistle blowing are not exhausted by examining its aim. Many moral philosophers have insisted that consideration of motives is relevant in assessing the morality of a person's action. Suppose that a potential presidential assassin attempts to push the president in front of a train. The president stumbles but does not fall in front of the train. As the president stumbles, the shot of another assassin (whose existence is unknown to the first) misses the president. Surely the action of the first potential assassin is not morally justified even though the act had good results. Surely the first potential assassin does not deserve the congressional medal of honor.

Now consider possible motives for whistle blowing. A desire to attract attention, to get ahead, to shift the focus away from one's genuine weakness, and a general propensity toward being a troublemaker all represent possible motives for whistle blowing, but obviously none of them passes the first justificatory test. A whistle blower's motive should be to protect the public interest. Anything less than that undercuts the justification of whistle blowing.

Yet another justificatory constraint is that the whistle blower exhaust all internal channels for dissent. Since the whistle blower does have an obligation of loyalty to his or her employer, he or she should—at least in normal circumstances—use the institutional mechanisms that have been created for the purpose of registering dissent with the policies or actions of the corporation. One can be cynical about such institutional mechanisms, but, as we have seen from the chapter on self-regulation, the modern corporation has good reasons for developing self-regulatory mechanisms that are indeed effective. In fact, two contemporary theorists have argued that

> The task of ethical management is to have anticipated the pressures which would give rise to the concealed and harmful practice, and to have helped create patterns of communication within the organization so that whistleblowing would not be necessary. The focus on attempting to assure protection for the whistle-blower is, from the point of view of managerial ethics, basically misconceived—the managerial task is to prevent the necessity of whistle-blowing.[3]

As such effective mechanisms develop, the whistle blower is under an obligation to use them.

Yet another element in justified whistle blowing refers to the evidential base on which the whistle blowing is done. Charges of immorality should be based on strong evidence. Definitions of what counts as strong evidence go far beyond the subject matter of this book. I rest content with the semilegal notion that the evidence should be strong enough so that any person in a similar situation would be convinced that the practice being protested is indeed immoral. We have already seen how the concept of the "reasonable man" functions in judgments of deceptive advertising. The "reasonable man" standard is also used in liability and negligence lawsuits; hence, we will let the concept suffice here.

Yet another requirement for justified whistle blowing focuses on the nature of the moral violation itself. First, the seriousness of the violation should be considered. Just as parents should only call the doctor when a child is seriously ill and not when the illnesses are minor, whistle blowers should only violate their obligation of loyalty to their employers for grave moral matters. Fastidiousness about moral matters is not a requirement for business ethics. Another element to be considered is how immediate the moral violation is. The greater the time before the violation is to oc-

---

[3] This quotation is from a discussion draft prepared for the Hastings Center Project on "The Teaching of Ethics" by Charles W. Powers and David Vogel, p. 40.

cur, the greater the chances that internal mechanisms will prevent the anticipated violation. In general, whistle blowing is more justified the more immediate the violation is. Finally, the violation should be something specific. General claims about a rapacious company, obscene profits, and actions contrary to the public interest simply will not do. Such claims must be backed up with identifiable examples—examples that will stand up under the other justificatory tests.

The fourth justificatory requirement enables us to return to the discussion of role morality that represented the focal point of Chapter 1. Some positions within the corporate structure have as part of their job description a concern with the morality of corporate actions. In some instances, the job is specified as being concerned with corporate responsibility—the ombudsman or the vice president for corporate responsibility serve as examples. In other cases, certain kinds of moral activities are the responsibilities of corporate personnel. Corporate auditors check on the legitimacy of expense account statements. Quality control personnel have special responsibilities concerning consumer safety. Other examples come readily to mind. When some moral matter is the specific assignment of an employee, that person has special responsibilities associated with that role. Where the corporate role gives an employee explicit responsibility for some matter with ethical dimensions, the corporation is normally committed to following the advice of the person given the responsibility. After all, failure to do so would create a serious ethical dilemma for the employee with the moral responsibility. If the corporation overruled the advice, the employee would either have to acquiesce in an activity that he or she has already determined to be illegal or immoral or he or she would have to blow the whistle.

Consider someone given responsibility for quality control. The effect of such role-related responsibilities is to reduce the stringency of at least some of the other justificatory conditions for acts of whistle blowing. A person assigned responsibility for quality regarding safety needs only very limited evidence to pull a product or even a product line. His or her suspicions about inferior products do not need to meet the reasonable man standard. His or her professional judgment is what is most important since the corporation assigned that person to that task.

Special responsibilities for moral matters are not limited to job descriptions created by the business institutions themselves. Where corporations make use of *professional* employees, there are certain moral obligations associated with the role of that profession. Often those obligations are spelled out in a professional code of ethics. The best known example is engineers. One provision of the code of the American Society of Civil Engineers is that an engineer "will use his knowledge and skill for the advancement of human welfare and refuse any assignment contrary to this goal." The National Society of Professional Engineers has a rather extensive code of ethics consisting of fifteen major sections. The society publishes the opinions of the society's Board of Ethical Review. The board considers actual cases and makes a judgment as to whether or not a member of the society would be or is in violation of the code if he or she acts in a certain way. Being a professional engineer binds those engineers to the code of conduct of the society and by implication binds the companies that employ these individuals as well. After all, in hiring a professional it is presumed that one wishes to employ a person who meets certain professional standards and, unless specified otherwise, an employer accepts all the standards of professional behavior for that profession. Can you imagine a company's explicitly indicating that it is appropriate to employ an engineer who meets all the standards of the profession except the ethical ones? I certainly cannot.

If we return to some of the case studies that opened this chapter, we see that some of the requested activities violate professional standards. A laboratory researcher cannot be asked to select the results of experimental work to favor a certain conclusion, since the function of a laboratory researcher is an impartial pursuit of the truth. Biased selectivity is contrary to the very purpose of scientific research. Similarly, the nurse in our example would violate the standards of the nursing profession if the dirty syringes were not reported. As the work force of American corporations contain a greater percentage of professionals, there will be an increasing number of employees within the corporation who have professional codes that regulate certain matters of business ethics. It seems to me that, if corporations want professional standards, they will have to accept the ethical standards of the profession as well. In this way, professional associations may serve as an alternative to self-regulation and government regulation to achieve greater corporate responsibility.

The final justificatory condition is more controversial and leads directly into a discussion of the relation of ethics and self-interest—the topic that both opened this chapter and concludes this book. The final justificatory condition is that whistle blowing have some chance of success. If there is no hope in arousing societal or government pressure, then one is needlessly exposing oneself and one's loved ones to hardship for no conceivable moral gain. It is not simply a matter of saying that an employee is not obligated to blow the whistle if there is no chance of success, but that whistle blowing that does have no chance of success is less justified, all things being equal, than is whistle blowing that does have a chance of success. The reader should note that I am not saying that such whistle blowing is never justified and hence should never be done. Sometimes such whistle blowing should be done if, for example, the violation is especially grave and the whistle blower's other personal obligations are few. On balance, however, given the dangers that personal whistle blowers run, the more likely the chances of success, the more justified the act of whistle blowing is.

Whistle Blowing and Self-Interest

The decision as to whether or not to blow the whistle, like the decision to commit civil disobedience, is seldom easy. One's loyalty is always under question. More important, one's job and hence one's livelihood is often at stake—and the loss of job is not confined to the company where the whistle blowing occurs. One's reputation as a whistle blower is usually a factor in not receiving the next job, even though such allegations are often hard to prove. The hard lot of the whistle blower has been described in several newspaper accounts and has received more extended coverage in Kenneth D. Walters, "Your Employees' Right to Blow the Whistle," *Harvard Business Review* (July–August 1975); Helen Dudas, "The Price of Blowing the Whistle," *The New York Times* magazine, October 30, 1977; and David H. Ewing, *Freedom Inside the Organization* (E. P. Dutton, 1977).

The fact that whistle blowing frequently has dire consequences for the whistle blower raises the question as to whether or not a person who knows of a moral violation on the part of the corporation has an *obligation* to blow the whistle. A similar dilemma occurs whenever an employer is ordered to do something immoral or illegal and is likely to lose the job if compliance is not forthcoming. As you may recall it is with just such a situation that I challenged the reader in the opening pages of this book. In that case, it is clear that, by blowing the whistle, the employee will lose his or her job. In that case, it certainly looks as if the channels are closed. Is the employee obligated to blow the whistle? Put in more abstract philosophical terms—are we always obligated to do what is morally appropriate regardless of self-interest? The "Why be moral?" question has sparked considerable philosophical debate. For some philosophers, once the morally appropriate action has been decided, there is no longer any question to be asked since by definition reasons of morality override reasons of self-interest. Most philosophers agree, however, that the question cannot be settled by definitional fiat. However, it is not obvious how such conflicts between morality and self-interest could be resolved. If moral reasons override prudential ones, one should whistle blow. One should refuse the immoral or illegal orders of a supervisor. If prudential reasons override moral ones, one should not whistle blow. One should not refuse the immoral or illegal orders of a superior. But which reasons override the other?

I suggest that this conflict has been resolved somewhat arbitrarily and fuzzily by social practice. Generally, moral reasons override prudential reasons, but where the damage to self-interest is especially serious, prudential reasons are *permitted* to override moral ones. A soldier is *not obligated* to throw himself on a grenade to save his fellows; there can be no obligation to give up one's life for morality. However, should a soldier choose to throw himself on the grenade, his action is highly moral. Indeed, philosophers have a name for such moral actions—supererogatory. Whistle blowing that threatens one's very livelihood is more like throwing oneself on the grenade than it is like following the ordinary rules of human behavior—don't lie, don't cheat, don't steal, and so on. Refusing to follow illegal or immoral orders is like whistle blowing in this regard. If I am correct in this comparative judgment, moral actions in cases in which one is likely to lose one's livelihood are supererogatory moral actions; they are not ordinary moral obligations.

But if these actions are not morally obligatory, how can society be protected from serious corporate wrongdoing? I believe the only reasonable answer to this question is to restructure business and social institutions so that these supererogatory moral acts no longer carry such severe personal penalties. The law should recognize constitutional rights in the workplace as well as in the other areas of life. Vogel and Powers' suggestions that corporate management protect whistle blowers also deserves serious study. It is in this vein of protecting whistle blowers that anonymity be obtained wherever possible. Under this view whistle blowing would have one characteristic that makes it very dissimilar from cases of civil disobedience. A requirement for justified civil disobedience is that the disobedient act be publicly and openly acknowledged. However, some have argued that the special circumstances surrounding whistle blowing justify omitting the openness requirement from the list of justificatory conditions. In cases of civil disobedience, the state itself is being challenged; in cases of whistle blowing, the public and hence the state is being protected from the immoral act of an institution within society. Hence, in the latter cases, it is in society's interest to promote whistle blowing. Relaxing the openness requirements is one way to promote this end.

The dangers of anonymity should also be mentioned, however. What is to protect a specific employer or indeed a whole company from unjustified charges of moral dereliction unless the accused can openly confront their accuser. Anonymity gives too much license to the accuser. Although the issue remains a matter of some debate, it should be pointed out that, as the protections for whistle blowers increase, the needs for anonymity decrease proportionally.

Of course one of the best protections for an employee is prudence in the selection of an employer. After all it is in a person's self-interest to seek an employer who has high moral standards and a company where those high moral standards are valued. No one wants to work for an unjust boss. A person who is consistently asked to perform actions contrary to his or her conscience may develop psychological problems or even physical illnesses. Finally, if one's boss behaves unethically in relations with others, he or she is likely to treat you the employee unethically as well. The message is clear. When considering an employer, consider ethical reputation as well as salary.

The discerning reader will note that this discussion of whistle blowing has shifted the "why be moral?" question from individuals to institutions. We have argued that in dire circumstances one cannot ask individuals to sacrifice their very livelihoods for morality. Rather, social institutions should be restructured so that such extreme individual sacrifices on behalf of morality are not needed.

Why Should Business Be Moral?

One answer to this question seems fairly straightforward. The corporation should be moral so long as acting morally is in the interests of the corporation. Moral behavior on the part of the corporation in such circumstances is rationally prudent behavior. In the literature of corporate ethics, many articles may be found that read like the admonitions of Epicurus against some of the less restrained hedonists. For example Aristippus the Cyrenaic advocated the pursuit of pleasure, now, with as much intensity as possible. But Epicurus knew that tonight's party was followed by tomorrow's headache and hence that restrained hedonism required only a cheese for sumptuous dining. Analogously, many corporate executives have lectured their counterparts on the virtues of deferred profit gratification. Low salaries and inadequate working conditions cut productivity. Ugly factories and an attitude of indifference toward the community in which one's plants are located generate hostility and a government climate not hospitable to business. Shoddy products ultimately drive the consumer away. In other words, the pursuit of the quick buck is not in the long-run interest of the firm. Since stable corporations need to be successful for the long term, "Look to long-run profits" is the official position of most corporate executives.

This appeal to enlightened self-interest is not sufficient for ensuring corporate behavior up to our moral standards. To see this, we need only draw a distinction between what is in the interest of a particular business and what is in the interest of business in general. We have already discussed an illustration familiar to economists and decision theorists that makes this point. As was pointed out in Chapter 5, the situation faced by steel companies is not unlike that faced by the prisoners in the so-called "prisoner's dilemma." It is in the long-term interest of the steel companies to install antipollution devices, but, in the absence of institutional arrangements that compel all steel companies to install the devices, it is in the self-interest of the individual companies not to install them. In general, there are many instances of activities that are in the long-term interest of business but are not in the long-term interest of an individual business firm unless that individual firm can be assured that all other firms will undertake similar activities.

There are escapes from the prisoner's dilemma situation, however.

We have already noted that the business community could use some form of self-regulation (adopt a code that requires the installation of antipollution devices), or it could simply agree to submit to government regulations on this matter. What is important here is the fact that corporate responsibility requires collective action. The independent action of one corporation will not do. Just as it is unreasonable to expect a whistle blower to blow the whistle when his or her livelihood is threatened, so the individual corporation would find it unreasonable to expect it to do the morally appropriate thing when its survival is threatened. Moral conduct in those cases would be supererogatory.

Recognition of the distinction between what is in the enlightened self-interest of an individual corporation and what is in the enlightened self-interest of the business community in general explains several interesting facts of corporate life.

First, it explains the reluctance of any corporation to act alone in meeting a requirement of morality that would significantly increase the price of its product or cut its profit significantly below the profits of its competitors. Such moral behavior would put the corporation at a serious disadvantage in retaining its customers or its stockholders. By the way, it will not do to say that customers will support such morally enlightened companies. For years service stations provided free mops, rest rooms, air for tires, and many other similar services. With the advent of self-service pumps, other stations without the amenities are successful. Not only do people not support the full-service stations, but they try to use the rest room facilities without buying anything.

Second, we see why the more successful (profitable) firms can afford to be moral. Firms operating on a very tight profit margin are in danger of not surviving. Firms with a comfortable profit margin are not running that danger. Any moral behavior that cuts profits will be accomplished more easily by firms with good profit margins than by firms with low profit margins. Hence we explain the popular business aphorism—a business can do good only by doing well. One also sees why business people insist that an ethical theorist cannot both attack profits as intrinsic evils and at the same time expect a corporation to be socially responsible. The more profitable a company is, the more responsible it can be. Morality is in the long-term interest of the corporation, but only if it can survive in both the short term and the long term.

In making these comments, I do not wish to give the reader the impression that whenever morality interferes with profit the business firm is justified in ignoring morality. As was indicated in Chapter 3, just as football teams are not justified in doing anything to win, businesses are not justified in doing anything to be profitable or even stay in business. As businesspersons are fond of pointing out, business involves risks; you can fail. But how seldom are the instances where businesspersons are good losers! Nonetheless, I am attempting to show some of the circumstances that make the practice of morality difficult and furthermore to delineate circumstances in which certain moral acts would be supererogatory. In this society we can try to adjust situations so that moral actions on the part of businesses and businesspersons would be more rather than less likely.

One situation deserves special comment, however. Some firms usually owned and operated by a few individuals have no interest in the long term. They can cheerfully quote Keynes, "In the long run we are all dead." A firm specializing in Nixon souvenirs would have been mistaken in taking the long-run point of view. There are many examples of enterprises where on rational self-interest grounds only the short run should be considered. Tonight's party is not followed by tomorrow's headache but by another party. Businesses in the entertainment industry, records, television, books, movies, nightclubs, toys, and games thrive on quick changes in fashion. The successful company gets on the fashion merry-go-round early and gets off early. What do you do with a million hula hoops when the fashion has passed by? The clothing industry and the securities industry must also pay considerable attention to the short run. Simply put, corporations, like people, know that the deferring of pleasure or greater profit is not always rational. Indeed many industries thrive on being successful in the short run. They either intend to make a sufficient killing so that the long run is provided for or to shift quickly from one short-term venture to another. Some businesses that thrive on maximizing in the short term are referred to both within and without the business community as fly-by-night operators. It is interesting to note that the response of "respectable" business executives to fly-by-nighters is not unlike that of "respectable" citizens to the excessively hedonistic or improvident members of the general community. There is something immoral about such behavior. What is needed, the corporations add, is something akin to the combination of law and morals that operates in the general society. Hence, respectable companies impress on the minds of their stockholders and the consuming public that their products are not shoddy, that their workers are not underpaid, and that they are taking positive steps to help solve society's problems. At the same time Better Business Bureaus are created and responsible government regulations are endorsed.

Yet why should the fly-by-nighters pay any heed to their more "respectable" colleagues? For these companies, the demands of morality (socially responsible behavior) clash with the demands of self-interest (prudence). In such cases of genuine conflict, why should these companies be moral? Moreover, why should companies that consumer demand forces to focus on the short run be concerned with long-run morality?

Worse questions are yet to come. An individual corporation may concede that morality (socially responsible behavior) is in the interests of the business community as a whole. However, the best interests of that corporation are achieved when the corporation pretends to be moral, and yet at the same time "cheats" whenever the manager thinks that he or she can get away with it. Success in that game will *maximize* the long-term interests of one's corporation. Kenneth Arrow puts it this way:

> *After all an ethical code, however much it may be in the interest of all, is, as we remarked earlier, not in the interest of any one firm. The code may be of value to the running of the system as a whole, it may be of value to all firms if all firms maintain it, and yet it will be to the advantage of any one firm to cheat, in fact the more so, the more other firms are sticking to it.*[4]

It is here that the clash between morality and self-interest is unambiguous. The attempt to reconcile the two is impossible. What can now be said on behalf of an affirmative business response to the "why be moral" question?

The Contract Analysis Again   The main step in providing an answer to the "why be moral" question is to return to the contractual basis on which business rests. As was argued in Chapter 2, the operation of a business, particularly when the business is a corporation, is not a matter of right. Robert A. Dahl has put the point this way:

> *Today it is absurd to regard the corporation simply as an enterprise established for the sole purpose of allowing profit making. We the citizens give them special rights, powers, and privileges, protection, and benefits on the understanding that their activities will fulfill purposes. Corporations exist only as they continue to benefit us . . . . Every corporation should be thought of as a social enterprise whose existence and decisions can be justified only insofar as they serve public or social purposes.*[5]

Actually, Dahl's quotation not only indicates that the relation between business and society is contractual but spells out the nature of that contract. The corporation must not only benefit those who create it, it must benefit those who permit it (namely, society as a whole).

But, of course, an individual corporation could still ask why it should keep its agreements if it can get away with breaking or evading them. After all, in a competitive situation, one ought to take advantages of opportunities and the opportunity to avoid or break the rules successfully

---

[4] Kenneth Arrow, "Social Responsibility and Economic Efficiency," *Public Policy*, Vol. 21 (Summer 1973), 315.

[5] Robert A. Dahl, "A Prelude to Corporate Reform," in *Corporate Social Policy*, eds. Robert L. Heilbroner and Paul London, (Reading, Mass.: Addison-Wesley Publishing Company, 1975), pp. 18–19.

is just another "lucky break" that should be capitalized upon. Naturally, such opportunities will not occur very often; usually, it is in the long-term interest of the firm to play by the rules (be moral). However, when long-term interest conflicts with morality, a corporation would be foolish to sacrifice its interests to morality, wouldn't it?

What can be said on the other side? Arguments from Chapter 3 have already shown that the success of the corporate enterprise itself depends on parties' keeping their agreements. The survival of the very corporation contemplating a violation of the rules depends on the general practice that corporations keep their contracts. If a corporation concedes this point, as I think it must, on what grounds can a corporation expect others to keep their agreements while it reneges on its. Now our potentially wayward corporation might respond that it is unique in some respect and hence immune from the general moral injunction to keep agreements. But how would such a uniqueness claim be justified? The other parties would have to accept it. Such an exemption would almost certainly not be granted. Indeed the decision of the corporation to clandestinely break the rules gives *prima facie* warrant to the claim that the corporation knows it could not *publicly* plead for an exception. Hence, a corporation that requires the general practice of rule keeping but that contemplates violating the rules when it is to its advantage to do so is being inconsistent and irrational. It accepts the necessity of keeping contracts and yet seeks to violate such a contract. It seeks to make an exception of itself without being willing to allow other competing corporations to do the same thing in similar circumstances. And surely that is inconsistent. And this type of inconsistency, when practiced, is what we mean by unfair. Benefiting from rules that one advocates but disobeys is a paradigm case of acting unfairly.

But suppose that our potentially wayward corporation is willing to subscribe to the rule: Corporations should keep their contracts unless they can successfully break or avoid them. Willingness to adopt this rule would avoid the charges of inconsistency. But what would a business world that adopted that rule be like? Would not such a world be very insecure and unstable? Relations among corporations and relations between corporations and their customers would resemble relations among suspicious and unfriendly nation states. The world of business would resemble the world of international relations, and surely that kind of instability is not advantageous to good business. Why should a corporation be moral?

1. Because usually it is in its interest. (prudence)
2. Because morality is in the interest of the corporate community in general.
3. Because each individual corporation agreed to behave morally.

4. Because to renege on its agreement and yet expect others to keep theirs is unfair.

5. Because to agree to a set of rules to govern behavior and then to clandestinely violate those rules is inconsistent.

6. Because to agree to a condition where business and businesspersons may break the rules if they can get away with it is to undermine the environment necessary for business.

Moral Practice in the "Real" World The argument given represents the final argument against those like Carr (Chapter 3) who argue essentially that business should put prudence ahead of morality when it can get away with it. It may be that some readers have been persuaded by the present analysis. Certain moral standards do underlie business practice, and individual businesses should adhere to those standards. However, whatever may be correct philosophically, the real world in which business must operate is characterized by some businesses' breaking the rules when they can get away with it. To operate on a high moral plane in the "real" world is to put one's firm at a disadvantage and hence to act "irresponsibly" in terms of profit maximization.

As a philosopher, I am in no position to make an accurate judgment on how business actually operates. However, it is my best judgment that, when corporations begin to take moral shortcuts, either the government steps in and further constrains business or a Hobbesian state of nature develops in which each business ends up trying to cut the throat of its competitors. Either result undermines the conditions of capitalism. There are many who have argued that capitalism contains within itself the seeds of its own destruction. Marx and Shumpeter are two of the most prominent examples. Let me add a final twist to the "seeds of its own destruction" theme. To the extent that corporations undermine the ethical foundation that make capitalism possible, they engage in behavior that will bring about their own destruction. I do not know how far current business practice departs from this ethical foundation. But I am convinced that business ethics is not the mere plaything of the public relations office. Rather, business ethics as characterized in this book is absolutely necessary for sound management; if capitalism is to survive, the pursuit of profit must be constrained by morality.

Index